Our Concrete Angels

By

Audrey Rose Addison

How blessed are those
Whose way is blameless
Who walk in the Law of
The Lord
(PS. 119.1)

Order this book online at www.trafford.com
or email orders@trafford.com

Most Trafford titles are also available at major online book retailers.

Print information available on the last page.

ISBN: 978-1-4120-6361-6 (sc)
ISBN: 978-1-4122-0100-1 (hc)
ISBN: 978-1-4122-0533-7 (e)

Trafford rev.   08/18/2016

www.trafford.com
North America & international
toll-free: 1 888 232 4444 (USA & Canada)
fax: 812 355 4082

Acknowledgements

My Husband

He stood beside me when I thought
no one else would. He made me
smile like no one else could. This
man I will cherish for the rest of my
life. This man who asked me to be
his wife.

I love You, **Parker**.

My Inspirations

My three children: **Parker Jr.**, **Amber
Renee'** and **Kayla**. They are my
reason for being.

My Siblings

We huddled together, quiet as a mouse.
Six lonely children, not making a sound.
We huddled together, all in one house.
Six lonely children, not to be found.

I dedicate this book to the strongest
people I know my brothers and
sisters:
**Carmen, Ceely, Cameron Jr.,
Cossette** and **Craig**.
I will love and need you always

Special Thanks To

I would like to thank a special lady who helped edit my book and taught me so much more about the art of writing. I also send my deepest gratitude to my therapist for taking my hand and guiding me through the darkest chapters. My heart is full with the warmest feelings for Parkland Hospital, not only for saving my life at three years old but allowing one of their professional people, fifty years later, to walk with me and validate my memory of pain and recovery. This is from my heart to yours.

Martina McBride, who my deepest heartfelt gratitude goes to. Her song, 'Concrete Angel' inspired me to gather the courage to write this book. I saw myself in this little girl. A child that the world forgot. My heart also goes out to the writer of this beautiful song. I hope one day to meet you both, but until then, please know that there is one little girl in this world that no longer feels forgotten, because of you. Words just aren't enough for me to express how I feel, so I hope you both know by naming my book 'Our Concrete Angels" you will feel how deep my gratitude goes. Thank you!

Prologue

"Big cities covered with concrete.
Walked on by adults too busy to
notice the cries of our little Angels."

I pushed the kitchen chair back away from the table almost knocking it over. Pages of my manuscript slid off the table onto the floor. I had to try and regain control. My hands are shaking as I let the screen door slam behind me. I walk aimlessly unaware of the beauty around me. Memories buried away in my subconscious struggled to maintain secrecy and at times frustrated accurate recall. While gazing out at the expanse of the blue shimmering lake, memories began a gradual flow back to me.

Bending down to the waters edge, I cup my hands and let the cool water cascade over my wedding rings. At the tender age of 17, my marriage to Parker offered me an unconditional love that has protected me now for 32 years. Our love is real! It is my life!

I owe it to our marriage to acknowledge and own the bitter experience of my childhood. I can deal with the memories. However, I wish. I can compartmentalize them into a sheaf of journal papers stuffed in the bottom drawer of my dresser, or burn them. It is all about choices.

It has just been four months ago when Parker and I moved from Dallas to Kingston, Oklahoma. The fine living, we had known disappeared with the loss of employment in the aftermath of September 11, 2001. We lost everything. I said a tearful goodbye to my sister, Ceely. This new, strange location made me feel lonely, and I mourned the life we had. Ceely and I shared a closeness we hadn't had since childhood, and I missed our conversations. My heart also aches at the thought of miles now between my children and me. Just the thought of not holding one of my grandchildren each day brings tears to my eyes.

But to my surprise, with the passing months, I find peace on the shores of Lake Texoma. It is strange that I had evolved to a point where I stopped pointing fingers. I cease blaming myself for what I deem stupid mistakes. I now realize that God led me here. God has offered me the comfort of solitude so I can hear and feel His wisdom. In the silence, I feel Him tell me I was so busy trying to rescue everyone around me that I neglected to appreciate the blessings He lavished on me. I began to feel more passion in my prayers and sought an even closer relationship with Him.

"Dear Lord, please show me what I need to do. If you are offering guidance, I am missing your message. Please open my mind, take away all these painful thoughts I am having and guide me. God, please help me."

Even as I pray, I feel a calmness come over me. Everything started to fall into place, and I began to think clearly. The beauty of Lake Texoma offers a serene environment to connect with an inner peace that only God can provide. This grace has brought me to a place where I feel inspired to write about my childhood. I know that for me to fully forgive, I need to face my memories, and find that little girl; the one I let die within in me at five years of age. I feel compelled to do this for every child who is forced to become an adult physically while clinging desperately to a child's way of thinking. Yes, I have to write this book! Even though what I write may hurt someone close to me, I have to try to stop the cycle of pain. If my story helps save one innocent child, it will be worth writing.

My eyes seek out the lake again. I slowly scan the smooth surface of the water. Gingerly, I step back from the edge and feel something hard move under my foot as sand pushes up between my toes. Nimbly I stand on one leg and pry a small shell from my left foot. Gently, while holding it in the palm of my hand, I run my fingernail over the surface. This tiny shell is different. Not like the one you would find on the seashore. No, more like one at the bottom of a fish tank. It is the size of a quarter. There are no distinctive colors, white with a touch of gray around its edge. I turn the shell over in my hand and gently pry it open. I note demur colors come to the surface with just a slight tilt of my hand. Colors softer than a rainbow- silvers, browns, and blacks. Very thin lines are fusing together as one. I caught my breath at the wonder of such harmony coming from one tiny shell. I then moved my hand sharply to the right, away from the brilliance of the sun and the lake. The charm of the shell vanished quickly. No color or allure. Like menacing thunderclouds, the inside turned ominous, changing to dark gray and then blackness. My first instinct was to drop it, but I force myself to remember the beauty it holds. I close my hand tightly around it and think how sad something as wondrous as this small shell has the power to make me feel so vulnerable. It reminds me of myself as a child. On the outside, I'm just another frail victim of society, but on the inside, I am so much more.

With a deep sigh, I sink to my knees. With eyes filled with tears, I wonder how I ever made it this far. Why didn't God take me when I was burned badly at three years old? Why didn't I end my life as a teenager when I thought my destiny was to be used and thrown away by the very people I thought loved me? My thoughts are taking me back to the anger I feel each time I confront the realization that the treatment I received from my parents wasn't normal. Parents are supposed to love and protect their children. I had tried all through my childhood to love my parents in spite of the horrors they inflicted. At their command, my siblings and I kept the good memories that were acceptable to society. We believed what we were told to believe, and lived in fear of their threats of abandonment.

I became aware of the water lapping at the end of my skirt. Slowly I rose to my feet and wiped away the tears while shaking the sand from my clothes. I feel the warmth of the sun on my face and know that God has returned strength and control to my body and soul. Clutching the small shell, I head back to the cabin. I step inside and immediately gather the scattered pages of my manuscript from the floor. I place them neatly on the table. Feeling stronger I place the shell next to my pen and paper, to remind me of how *God's Grace* inspired me to find it. I scan the pages until I find where I stopped writing. A strange feeling takes over me. My stomach feels like a thousand butterflies have been let loose in it and the pages seem to be blurring. God is in control! The barriers to those secret hiding places fell away, and I view myself as being only three years old as the memories flow unimpeded from my fingertips onto the page...

Chapter 1

God blesses those whose hearts are
Pure, for they will see God
(Mathew 5:8)

I carefully crawl out of bed and run to
the bathroom, which isn't easy since I share
a bed with my two older sisters. The old
wood floor was cold on my tiny feet. I raise
my long nightgown, one I had so proudly
put on by myself the night before. I am
careful not to let it fall into the potty. The
gown had belonged to my sister Ceely.
She's just a little over a year older than
me. I got all her clothes as she grew out
of them. Of course, she receives our older
sister, Carmen's hand me downs. No one
gets mine because the next in line was
Cameron Junior, our little brother and I think
he would have looked a little funny in girl's
clothes. I sit there humming a song kicking
my legs back and forth. Finished I jump
off the potty. Feeling the cold on my feet
again, I wish I had remembered my socks.
My gown falls back into place as I run down
the hall past my parents' room. I try to be

very quiet so that I don't wake Junior. He sleeps in the room with them. I giggle when I think of my little brother. I'm the *Big Sister* now. I am much older than him.

He's only a Year and a half, and I'm a whole three years old, so that makes me bigger. The floor gets warmer, the closer I get to the living room. Oh, yea! Daddy put fire on the stove. The heater in this room is just my size, an old open type with bricks that heat up when you light them with a match. I slowly get closer until I feel the heaters warmth on my body. Just as I feel my cheeks heat up, I hear the pitter-patter of tiny feet. I turn and see Junior wobbling toward me. I raise a finger to my lips and tell him he has to be quiet. My little brother starts running to the heater. I shut the door and run after him. He loves to play chase, and so do I. Just as I run in front of the heater the bottom of my gown burst into flames.

The next thing I remember is standing beside my parent's bed screaming. Daddy jumps out of bed and throws a blanket on me, patting me all over. I'm hot, so hot. Mommy is screaming into the phone. Men come and put me in a big truck with lights.

The last thing I remember is looking for Junior. Everything is dark.

When I wake up, I realize I'm in a bed in a big room. Everything seems white. People with white masks on are talking and rushing around me. Some are staring at me and whispering to each other. I feel scared. I feel no pain just heat, and I can't stop shaking. People in white are trying to get the blanket off; that Daddy covered me with, it's stuck to me. A lady in white is pouring water on me. The blanket starts to peel away. I feel nothing. Now I see only shadows. I can't open my eyes. The voices are going away too. My eye's feel heavy. I still feel nothing.

I wake up screaming. *Mommy! Daddy! Help! I can't move. My arms are tied down. Where am I? Where is my bed? Where is Junior? Mommy! Daddy! Please help me! Why aren't any words coming out of my mouth?* Oh good, there's Daddy. He's walking toward me. Daddy looks like he has been crying.

Mommy is yelling at a man in white by the door, "Doctor you have to move her away from the window. She has pneumonia, and there are ants getting on her burns!" Mommy is crying now.

Daddy gives me a sad look and says he needs to talk to the doctor. He walks over to where Mommy and the man in white are.

He holds Mommy as the doctor is telling her, "There are no private rooms in the hospital for your child Mrs. Addison. She has to stay in this ward. Besides Chester Clinic is not a charity hospital. We will be transferring her to Parkland Memorial Hospital as soon as possible. All I can say now is that you should start praying for your little girl. That may be the only hope of survival she has." After that, the doctor just shook his head and walked out.

Daddy said, "No, we're not going to lose her." He walks over to my bed and drops to his knees. I know my Daddy is praying. Mommy has her hand on Daddy's back. Her eyes are closed. *Pain, why can't I feel the pain?*

It's morning, but I can't see very good. Everything seems fuzzy. *What's on my face? It feels heavy and hot.* A nurse comes in and tells me I am going to a new hospital today.

She says, "Now sweetie stop crying. You're okay. Please stop kicking, honey. You're going to hurt yourself. Don't pull on the bandages around your face, honey.

You have to have these on to protect you. Someone help me. Hurry!" Now there are more people here. They are holding me down.

"No, no don't stick me again. Oh please, help me, it hurts! I can feel it, and it hurts! Stop!"

They are rolling my bed out of my room. There are lights on the ceiling. They seem to be passing over my head fast. *Where are Mommy and Daddy? Why aren't they here? I can see two big doors.*

The nurse says, "We are going to put you in an ambulance now, everything is going to be fine. You are probably getting sleepy, and that is okay." She was right. My eyes started to close, and that's all I remember.

Daddy is standing next to my bed. He kisses me and smiles. "Audrey, how do you like your new room? It's a lot bigger than your old one, huh? Honey, you're at a new hospital now. They will be in here in a minute to give you some medicine. I know you don't like shots, but honey they have to give them to you so you can get better."

"Daddy, no more shots! They hurt me." I'm crying and looking around the room at the same time.

Yeah, this room is nicer. I can see better too. Not clear, but a little better. I look down at myself and think of the snowman Daddy helped us build at Christmas. There is white stuff wrapped all around my body. Daddy says it's called gauze. I don't know what that means, but I do know I don't like it. Mommy and Daddy look funny too. They look like that doctor all in white, and they have white masks too. More people in white are coming into my room.

"Oh no, please don't touch me! No! No! I want my Daddy."

People are holding me down again. "Daddy, where are you?" They try to stick me with needles. They tell me it's for my good.

"Oh! Mommy, Daddy, help me! Please stop them! It hurts! Ouch, ouch, ouch! They are hurting me!" My screams stopped as my body stopped feeling and I went to sleep.

I know I have been in the hospital for a long time, but I don't know how long. They're telling me I will have to have another operation tomorrow. At the beginning of my treatment, I would fight the doctor that had to give me a shot with a needle. It would take a lot of nurses to hold me down while they gave me shots and took off the gauze from my body.

Now I'm used to it. I know it wouldn't make any difference if I scream and kick, they will hurt me. They have to so I can heal, but it doesn't make it any better. I can hear voices coming from the hospital hallway outside my room. Daddy walks in with a man dressed in black, like the man in the church.

"Hi, Daddy, who's he?" My finger shakes as I point at the man.

"Audrey, this is the minister from the hospital's church. He wants to talk to me for a minute." Daddy keeps looking down. I nod and turn on my side as best I can. They sit down in chairs next to my bed and start talking about me as if I'm not there.

Daddy says, "She has to have another operation tomorrow. The Doctors will remove the good skin from the back of her legs and down her back. She's so very small. They have done over 100 skin grafts, and not one of them has taken. Many people have donated their skin for her, but the doctors say her body keeps rejecting the skin. They said the procedure for using the patient's skin has never been tried before. Audrey will be their first attempt at this but it is also her only chance of survival, and that's a very small chance."

The room is quite. I hear my Daddy crying. The man takes a book from his pocket and tells Daddy to pray with him. They walk over to my bed and kneel down.

I look at Daddy and say, "You're scaring me.?" He takes my hand and says he loves me; then they pray. I can't make out what the man is saying.

It sounds like he is whispering until he says, "Amen." He smiles at me and says, "Audrey you are a very brave little girl." Daddy walks him out of my room.

I cry, "Please, don't leave me, Daddy. I'm afraid of being by myself."

Daddy comes back and brushes away my tears. In a shaky voice, he says, "I will never leave you, Audrey."

"Daddy, I don't want another operation. It hurts so badly. I don't want to hurt no more." I hold on to Daddy's hand.

"Please Daddy, just let me die! Tell them to leave me alone!" I scream.

Daddy takes my hand. He is crying too. He says, "The family can't live without you, Audrey. Everything is going to be okay. Don't talk like that again. Go to sleep, honey. I will be right outside the door if you need me. You know I can't stay with you at night, but I promise I won't leave.

I look at him and say, "I don't want no more shots. I don't want them to peel the white stuff off my body no more. I don't want to hurt no more!" Daddy looks at me and sighs. He hangs his head and walks out the door.

I lay there crying. Maybe I will pray to Jesus. Daddy says he can hear us when we pray. Daddy says he lives in a place called Heaven, where everyone goes when they die so that they can be happy. I put my hands together, close my eyes, and began.

Please baby Jesus take me to Heaven with you. That's where my Daddy says you live. I don't want to be here anymore. I hurt so bad.

When I open my eyes, I see a man standing next to my bed. He's here. It's Jesus. I know because his picture hangs on the wall at our house. Except it's just the top part of him, and I can see the wall through him. I'm not afraid. He makes me feel safe. I don't hurt, and I'm not scared. I just feel safe. He is talking to me. His mouth doesn't move, but I know what he is saying. I don't know how I can understand him, but I just do.

He says, "*Audrey you will live. You will soon forget the pain never to recall it. It is not the time for you to die yet. I cannot let that happen. Believe in me, because I am Jesus, Son of God. I will always protect you.*"

The next morning when I wake up, I remember. I try to tell the doctors that Jesus came and visited me last night. They smile and say how lucky I am to have seen him, but they need to get me ready for my operation, like so many times before. Daddy walks into the room. One of the doctors says everything is going to be all right and this time the surgery will work.

Daddy holds my hand and smiles. I look up at him and say, "I know it will be all right, too. Jesus told me so."

I tell him what happened after he left last night. Daddy smiles and says, "I'm sure he did, honey."

The next thing I know the big cup is put over my face. I always fought to keep it away from me, but today I'm not going to fight. I know I am safe. I'm not afraid anymore...

Chapter 2

The time has come for you to hear,
what she says with just a tear. The time
has come for you to be near, to take
away all her fears."

I look up from my coloring book as Daddy walks into the room. It's been a long time since the operation that saved my life. The doctors call me their, *miracle patient.* Daddy calls me his, *miracle child.* They always smile when I tell them Jesus helped them save me. I watch my door all the time now waiting for Daddy or Mommy. One of them always comes in just before I have to go to what they call therapy. It's usually Daddy. I call it the *Angry Waters.* It's always bubbling, and it makes me angry.

"Hi Daddy, where's Mommy?" I asked looking at the door expecting her to be standing there.

"Hello, my Little Miracle Child. She had to work this morning." He says, looking away from me.

"Daddy, Mommy is always working. It makes me sad when Mommy doesn't come.

"We have to get you ready for the pool, baby. I know. I know you don't like going through that, but you have too. They have to change your dressings, or you will get sick again."

"Okay, Daddy," I put my crayons and book on my tray.

"Daddy when are you bringing the kids to see me?"

He smiles and carefully puts me into the chair with wheels. "They will be here next week, Audie. Remember we are going to have your Birthday. Granddaddy and Grandmother will be here too." He said this with a big smile. I love it when my Daddy smiles. He frowns too much lately.

"Will I have balloons and cake and ice cream? Chocolate, Daddy I want chocolate everything. Oh and presents and games. Will we get to play games?"

I put my head back and looked up at him as he pushes me down the long gray hallway. He's smiling again and shaking his head. A nurse walks up to us.

She says with a smile, "I didn't think this day would ever come. It is good to see you so happy."

Daddy stops and lowers himself in front of me. "Now Audrey, slow down. You're getting yourself all worked up. We don't want you to hurt yourself, honey. Yes, maybe you can have all those things at your party. Now don't pout, but we have to ask the doctor about the games, okay? After all, this is a Hospital baby, and you can't move around a lot yet."

"Okay, but the other kids can. Can't they?"

"We'll see, but don't be upset if they say no, okay?" Daddy pushes me again. I wonder if he's mad.

We were in the room where the bubbling water is. I wrinkle up my nose. I can always smell this room long before I get there. Daddy sits down next to me and takes my hand in his.

He said very quietly like he doesn't want anyone to hear him. "Listen, sweetheart; this will be over soon. You have been so strong and brave. Do you know you have been here for over a year? "Of course, you don't. Well, that's a long, long time. The doctors have to be sure the burns heal before you can go home, and they are healing very well."

The doctor who always puts me in the water walks up. He says to Daddy, "We're ready for her."

"Oh, I don't like this part. I know it's going to hurt." Slowly they lower me into the water. I have to sit forever it seems. Daddy always holds my hand and talks to me.

He asks, "What's wrong, honey? Do you need us to take you out?"

"No Daddy, you don't have to take me out this time. The water isn't hurting me like it did before. Does that mean I'm getting better?" Daddy and the doctor look at each other.

The doctor smiles and says, "That's what it means. Audrey, you're getting better every day. Sweetheart, this whole Hospital is proud of you."

More surprising was when they peeled the bandages off of me it doesn't hurt as bad. Putting the bandages back on still hurt. It's okay since I only have to go through this once a day now instead of twice.

"Come on, Audrey. It's time to go back upstairs to your room." Daddy puts me in my chair and too fast we are back in my room.

"I need to go home now, honey. Grandmother is watching the kids, and it's getting late." Daddy sounds sad again.

"Bye Daddy. See you tomorrow. I love you." I watch him walk out the door and stop to talk to a nurse. She comes in and asks if I would like to see the new babies.

"Sure," I say with a huge smile.

I'm very excited at this moment. Today is my birthday. The nurses are here decorating my room for my birthday party. I can't wait for everyone to get here. My visit to the *Angry Waters* are over, and the nurse says I don't have to have any more shots today. I know it's because of my birthday, and the shots make me sleepy.

"You know it's not right for a princess to sleep through her birthday," the nurse says as she puts me in my chair. I don't tell her, but nothing could make me sleep today.

They're here; they're here.

Ceely ran up to my chair and said, "I made you this cake. It's all chocolate inside. It's a clown, see."

"It's the most beautiful cake I have ever seen, and it has a big number four candle on it."

"You made this all by yourself? I like it, and it's chocolate inside? Thank you, I'm so glad Y'all came." With a big smile on my face, I look around the room.

"Where's Mommy? Why isn't she here? She told me she would come. She just told me the other day that she wouldn't have to work and that she would be here Daddy, and where's Junior?"

Daddy told Carmen and Ceely to put the presents on the stand next to my bed.

Then he turns to me, "I'm sorry baby, but Momma stayed home with Junior. He isn't feeling well, and we couldn't take a chance on you getting sick. Besides, look who's here."

My Grandparents walk in and my birthday party starts. Everyone sings *Happy Birthday* to me, and we play a few quiet games; after everyone leaves, I cry and cry. I miss my family so much. I want to go home.

The nurse comes in and holds my hand and asks, "Why are you crying, sweetie? Do you hurt somewhere?

"No, I'm sad. I want to go home. Was I bad? Is that why I got hurt and had to come here?" I try to stop crying but I can't.

"No, no sweetheart. Bad things just happen sometimes. It isn't your fault. Hey, give me that beautiful smile. Come on, I know it's there. Aren't you the *birthday girl*? Did you have a good time?"

I can't help it. I just can't stop crying, as I blubber, "I want to go home."

"Baby, I'm sorry, but I'm going to have to give you a shot to help you sleep, okay? We can't have you upset like this."

I just look at her. I don't care anymore. There are bruises on my behind from shots; they have to find other places to stick me, but tonight I just don't care.

Mommy came with me to my therapy today. The doctor says I only have a couple more to go. That makes me happy because I will be going home soon. Back in my room, there is another bed. Mommy asks the nurse if someone is moving in with me.

The nurse says, "Yes, another little girl will be here this afternoon. Audrey, she is very sick like you were when you first came. You have to be careful and not talk to her too much, okay?"

All I can think is, *yeah! I'm going to have company*. "Oh yes, I will be quiet. I'll just talk a little. When is she coming?"

The nurse smiles and says she will be here soon. It seems to take forever. Mommy has been gone a long time, and she still isn't here. Finally, here they come. I'm sad for her, though; she's like I was before. She still had lots of white bandages on, and she can't get out of bed. Her bed is different too. It has a big plastic sheet hanging over it, and she's under it. *I wish everybody would leave so I can talk to her. She looks scared.*

I guess I fell asleep waiting because the next thing I knew Daddy was waking me up, and it was morning.

"Wake up sleepy head and eat your breakfast." He kisses me on my cheek.

"Daddy, I have a new girl in my room. She's my friend, but Daddy why does she have that plastic thing over her bed? We didn't get to talk yet because they took too long last night. Where is she?" I pointed at her bed, but it was empty.

"Shhh- don't worry, hon, she will be back. I met her Mommy this morning. She had to go for some tests. You don't remember, but you had one of those plastic things too. They're called *oxygen tents*. They help your breathe." Daddy spreads jelly on my toast as he talks.

The door to my room opens, and there she is. They brought her back in bed. I watch them pick her up and put her back under the tent.

Daddy asks the doctor how she's doing, and he says, "Not too well."

It's been days since Jessica, that's my new friend's name, was put in my room. We talk a little, but she tires fast. She is seven years old. Her Mommy and Daddy are here all the time. They're nice, but they are sad too.

I ask my Daddy one day why her skin is black? He smiles and says, "Honey, all I can tell you is that God made us in all different colors. When you get older; you will meet people of many different colors."

I opened my eyes wide, and my mouth flew open, "Daddy you mean there are people who are blue, green and purple? Oh, I wish I were purple instead of pink." Jessica's Daddy hears us talking and he winks at my Daddy.

"When you get home I will show you some different color people in a book I have. They live all over the world, and some speak a different language than us." Daddy is always showing us pictures in books.

I walk to Jessica's bed and tell her about the birthday party I had.

Jessica says, "I wish I could have been in the room with you. It sounds like you had a lot of fun. My Daddy says I should be home by my birthday. I hope so."

Jessica starts coughing so I have to move away from her bed so that the doctors can get to her. Daddy says he has to go.

"C'mon honey, let's get you back into bed. Mommy will be here in the morning to go to therapy with you." He kisses me on my head and quietly leaves the room.

I wake to the sound of beeping noises coming from Jessica's side of the room. I try to raise and see Jessica, but there are doctors all around her bed.

One of the doctors is talking fast. "Get the oxygen mask back in place. Turn her to her right side. Now get her to Operating Room 1. Stat!" The doctor hurries out of the room.

"What's happening? Is something wrong with Jessica?

One of the nurses helping the doctor comes over to my bed. "Shhh honey, everything is fine. We have to take Jessica to another room. She's having trouble breathing. You go back to sleep." The nurse tucks me in and goes to help push Jessica's bed out the door.

"Wait! Bye, Jessica. I'll be here when you get back." Where are they taking Jessica, I feel scared. I want my Daddy.

The next morning, as Mommy and I are coming back from therapy Daddy, is standing by the door to my room.

"Hi Cameron, what's wrong? Why are you here? Who's with the kids?" Mommy is asking too many questions. I am just glad Daddy is here.

"First things first. Good morning, Audrey. It looks like things went well today. You got a kiss for me?" Daddy bends down to my chair and kisses him on the cheek. He takes my chair and rolls me next to my bed.

He starts talking to Mommy while lifting me into bed. "Well, to answer your questions, Carly. The kids are with your Mother, and I'm here because the doctor called and gave me good news and some sad news. I thought it would be better if I came here and talked to you both instead of calling."

"Why didn't the doctor just come up and talk to me? Did you tell him I was here with Audrey today? Oh, never mind, what did he say?" When Mommy was upset, she puts her hands on her hips, and her voice sounds different.

"Here, hon," Daddy was patting the bed next to me.

"Come over here and sit on the bed by Audrey." He waited while Mommy seated herself. "Now, for the good news. Dr. Potter said Audrey gets to go home soon. Maybe within three days, if all her tests come back good."

All I hear is, *I get to go home. I get to go home. Yea!* "Tomorrow Daddy? I get to go home tomorrow?"

"No honey, not tomorrow. Three tomorrows. The doctor says they are going to take off the rest of your bandages in the morning and see how you do. As long as no infection sets in you'll be fine." He looks at Mommy, "Carly, he also said they are amazed at how well Audrey healed after they grafted her with *her skin*." Daddy and Mommy looked at me. They both are smiling.

"Well with all the people praying for her she had to get well." Mommy reaches down, pats my head and hugs me.

I look over to Alicia's bed to see if she is back. "Daddy, why hasn't Jessica came back? I have to tell her I'm going home."

Daddy takes my hand and says, "Remember I have some sad news too. Oh Dear God, how do I do this. Baby, Jesica isn't coming back. She's gone to be with God in heaven. She couldn't breathe anymore, honey. She was just too tired."

"You mean Jesus came and seen her last night but instead of telling her she was going to live she died and went with him? Daddy, I didn't get to tell her goodbye."

"Baby, I don't know. Maybe God knew she wasn't strong enough to go through what you did. Audrey, it's not our place to question Him; someday we all will be in heaven, and you will see Jessica again, I promise."

Mommy looks angry, "Cameron! You shouldn't make her promises that you can't be sure of."

Daddy turned to Mommy and said, "Carly, it's called, Faith, and I know we will see Jessica in Heaven one day."

Mommy says she had to go to work. Daddy asked her to call grandmother and ask if she could stay with the kids a little longer. Mommy looked upset but said she would. Daddy stays with me the rest of the day.

Hooray, I go home today! I get to walk down that long gray hallway and out the door.

"I can walk, Daddy. I want to walk to the car. I don't want to get back in that chair."

"C'mon hon, this will be the last time. The doctor says you must. Hop in."

Daddy, I think I will always remember this room and Jessica." I feel sad, but happy at the same time.

Daddy stops my chair where the nurses work and signed some papers. One of the nurses tell Daddy they are going to miss me, but they are happy for me to be going home.

"Here you go, honey. We bought this for you to remember us. We will miss your happy little face so much."

It was a pink teddy bear wearing a suit like the nurses and it has a lot of names written on it. I love it.

"Thank you." I hug it close to me as daddy pushes me down the hallway.

I try to look back, but all I can see is the long gray hallway. I watch the bright lights pass over my head as Daddy pushes me to the elevator.

Daddy softly whistles a tune while we wait. I watch as the big doors open. Once inside I get a funny feeling in my stomach when the elevator drops. I look around in wonder when the doors clank open once more. People I don't know wave to us as we walk through the lobby. I'm amazed at how big everything is, and for the first time I see what the hospital looks like beyond my room. That funny feeling comes back to my stomach as Daddy lifts me into the car. *I'm going home!*

Chapter 3

"Sticks and Stones
May break your bones,
But words will forever hurt you."

One year has passed since I left the hospital. I'm five now. We recently moved to California, and I am starting Kindergarten. We live down the street from my Aunt Reba and Uncle Adam. They're my favorite Uncle and Aunt. Loraine, Ladonna, and Lily are their daughters. Loraine and I are very close in age, and we do everything together

A couple of weeks ago both of our Grandparents came for a visit. Our Grandmothers are sisters, so they usually take vacations together.

While my Grandparents are here visiting, they are going to *Disneyland*, but they said they would only take two of us kids with them. *Oh please, let it be me. Please, please, please!* My Grandmother said they were taking Carmen and Ceely, but they would bring me something back. I stood in the driveway crying as Granddaddy back the car out to leave. It isn't fair. I never get to do nothing.

Daddy took my hand and pulled me back to the house and tries to explain, "Audrey, they couldn't afford to take all you kids. We thought it would be easier for them to take Carmen and Ceely because they're the oldest. You can go next time; besides, we'll do something fun too."

I went into the house and stomped into the bedroom I now share with three sisters. While I was in the hospital my little sister Irene was born, so now there were five of us kids. Oh, why did I have to have so many brothers and sisters?

Daddy and Mommy took the rest of us kids down to my Aunts house. The adults played dominos, and we played outside. That was fun too, but I wish I were at *Disneyland*. When Carmen and Ceely got back from *Disneyland* they brought us all presents, so I guess it's all right I didn't get to go.

I start to school today. I'm so nervous and afraid. Yesterday Daddy said I would have to ride the bus home from school by myself, so he drove Carmen, Ceely and me there and then drove us back, so we would know our way home once the bus dropped us off. Now as Daddy pulls up in front of the school, I realize I'm not just afraid anymore I don't want to go. The school building looks so much bigger, and there are kids everywhere.

"Go on Audrey, hop out. You don't want to be late your first day" Daddy's voice snaps me out of my feelings of panic.

"I changed my mind I don't want to go. Just take me back home, okay?" I was shaking.

Daddy rolls his eyes and says, "Carmen help her out. Audrey go with your big sister now! I don't have time for this I have to go to work."

Carmen walks me to my classroom. Before leaving she says, "Be a good girl and just do what the teacher says and you will be okay. I'll see you after school."

She was right I learn real fast the kids that didn't listen got in trouble, so I sat very quietly and was a good girl. The only thing I don't like is we have to take a nap. I'm not a baby. I don't take naps anymore, but in school, I will cause the teacher says so.

Yea! A bell just rang, and the teacher says it's time to go home. My teacher is nice. She's making sure I get on the right bus. I'm so glad this day is over, and I can go home. I have to tell Momma and Daddy that this school isn't for me. They treat you like a baby, and I didn't learn anything. *Hey, wait a minute. The bus is moving. Where are my sisters? I'll just have to tell the bus driver he can't leave yet.* I stand, the bus driver yells for me to sit down. I flop back into my seat, scared to death. Before I know it, the driver says this is my stop. I pick up my bag and run off the bus. I stop and watch the bus pull away. Nervously, I look up and down the street. I'm lost, this isn't my stop. *Wait a minute is that the alley that leads to our house? Yes, this is it.* I know my house is behind one of these fences, but the fences are all made of wood, and they are tall. It seems like I have been walking up and down this alley for hours. I start crying and scream out for my Mommy and Daddy.

"I'm lost! Will someone please help me?"

Turning to look behind me I see Daddy stop his car at the end of the alley. I run as fast as I can right into his arms. He says I will never have to ride that school bus again, but he doesn't agree with me about not going to school. He says I have to go; something about *the Law*, and that I would get used to it. I agree to give it one more chance.

Well, I guess I like some stuff about school. What I don't like is these two boys and a girl in my class. They like to make fun of me. They say I'm too short to be in school; that I looked like a *midget*. I don't know what a *midget* is; I know it must be bad because they always laugh at me when they say it. Today, while playing on the monkey bars I turn upside down, and my dress falls over my head. I hear the girl start screaming and see her pointing at me. *Why is she pointing at me? I didn't do anything to her?*

Still screaming she says for me to get away from her, "you're scary, go away! What's wrong with you?" She runs to the teacher.

Running after her I yell, "No I'm not! There's nothing wrong with me!"

The teacher takes the little girls hand, asks what's wrong? "She has something ugly on her legs, see." As the girl talks my teacher motions for me to come to her.

As I follow my teacher back to the classroom, I hang my head feeling confused.

"Audrey, do you have scars on your legs? Here honey, let me see." I lift my dress. The teacher makes a sad face.

She is just looking at my legs. If she saw the rest of my body, she would probably agree with my classmates that I was *scary*.

"I got burned when I was three. I didn't mean too." I say as I lower my skirt.

"Of course, you didn't Audrey. It wasn't your fault. Honey, don't turn upside down on the monkey bars, unless you have pants on, okay? Your scars frighten the kids. They don't understand." She gave me a hug.

Back in the classroom, my teacher tried to explain to the kids why I had scars on my body. "Class when Audrey was younger she got burned really bad, so now she has scars on her legs. Don't be afraid there's nothing wrong with her. It was just an accident, and she got hurt. What happened to Audrey is why kids should never play with fire. It's very dangerous and as you can see will hurt you." She then raised my skirt and showed them my burns on my legs.

For the first time, I realized I was different, and it hurt. It hurt worse than all the pain I had suffered while I was in the hospital. That day some of the kids started calling me names. I was hurt and confused. I still don't understand why I'm scary. Well, I will play by myself from now on.

When I get home, I tell daddy what had happened.

"Honey, kids can be mean. Just ignore them if you can. There is nothing wrong with you. You are a beautiful girl."

"Okay Daddy, but it still hurts." Lowering my head, I turn and go toward my room.

"Hey, how about us going out back and start teaching you to ride that bicycle?"

"Okay, Daddy I'll race you there." I was already halfway to the back door.

My first bike ride was no different than any other way daddy taught me to do things. He put me on it, gave me a little shove, and down the alley I went. Daddy was yelling for me to put my feet on the pedals, but I couldn't. The bike was going too fast. The pedals are just spinning. I can see that I am going to end up in the middle of the street below. The next thing I know I am being pulled from the bike. Setting me down with a hard thud, Daddy runs out into the street and grabs the bike just as a car passes.

Mommy, comes running down the alley screaming, "Cameron, what were you thinking? She could be killed. Are you out of your mind?" Mommy takes my hand and pulls me back to the house.

"Audrey, you are not to get back on that bike again. Do you hear me?" Momma has me by both arms shaking me.

"Yes Momma, but don't be mad at Daddy. He's just trying to teach me to ride. The bicycles got those extra wheels on it. I promise not to go near the street again." Momma gives me one of her looks she always gives when I upset her.

"Audrey, do as I say. You are not to get on that bike again." She went into the house letting the screen door slam behind her.

I was waiting on the porch when Daddy walks up with the bike.

He gives me a wink and says, "Guess I better go in and face the music. I'll be out in a minute, and we will go over bike safety. Don't frown, Audrey. I will teach you to ride when Momma is at work, but remember it's our secret, okay?"

Three weeks later, keeping my promise to Momma I stayed away from the street, but I'm getting good at riding my bike too.

Daddy lost his job again, so we are staying with my Aunt and Uncle for now. The screen door opens and slams shut. We all look up from the table where Daddy has just set us for dinner. Momma slowly looks around the table at each one of us.

She then turns to Daddy and says, "Cameron, you were supposed to pack today. Where are the boxes? Did you call and rent a trailer?"

"C'mon Carly, let's go out back. Kids eat your dinner and then get ready for bed." He then turns and walks out the back door.

As one we run for the window to listen to Momma and Daddy talking. None of us knew we were moving. Not even Ceely, who always knows stuff before the rest of us kids. Daddy lit a cigarette and sat down on the steps. Momma was standing over him frowning. Oh, I know that look, Daddy is in trouble.

"Cameron, you know we have to leave. It was nice of your brother to let us stay, but we have worn out our welcome. For *God's sake*, we have eight kids in a three-bedroom house and five of them are ours. Cameron, you don't have a job, nor is there any prospects of one. We can't afford to stay here any longer." Momma slumps in a lawn chair and throws her head back.

"I know Carly, you're right, but I don't see how moving back to Texas is going to help. The kids are happy here with their cousins."

"Oh *Jesus*, Cameron! Are you not hearing a word I'm saying? You do not have a job. You haven't even looked for one. All I asked you to do is get us ready to leave, while I work and get the money together. Well Cameron, maybe you will understand this. In two days we leave for Dallas, rather you're ready or not I am taking the kids and leaving."

Momma haltingly raises herself from the chair and walks toward the front yard. At the gate, she turns back to Daddy. "Cameron, you know you have a better chance of getting a job in Dallas; besides Mom and Dad are helping us get back there. They want the kids home."

Carmen, my oldest sister, sits back down at the table first. Everyone else but me follows her. All the kids are talking at once. Carmen and Ceely are mad. They are saying Daddy always makes us move because he won't work. Carmen says she ain't leaving, and Ceely is arguing with her that she has to. I turn from the window and scream for them to shut up.

"Y'all don't know what you're talking about it ain't Daddy's fault that he can't get a job. It's this stupid place's fault. Look at Daddy; he looks so sad. It ain't any bodies fault. Oh, I hate everybody." I turn to run out of the room and run right into Mommas' leg.

"Okay, kids that's enough, put your plates in the sink and go to bed. Be happy that you get to be with your Grandparents again." Turning to my cousin Momma continues, "Loraine, you put your sister Lily to bed. Then you and Ladonna can wait up for your parents."

All five of us kids slept on a pallet in my Uncles living room. I can hear Mommy and Daddy arguing. Momma says we can't bring our dog, Nicky, with us. She says we can't afford to. Someone sniffles, so I look over at Ceely. She is staring up at the ceiling. I look toward Carmen. She has her face buried in her pillow. Her shoulders are shaking. I reach over and hug Carmen. She loves our dog.

Here we go, moving again. I guess we should be used to it. Oh well, we will be with Grandmother again. I've missed her so much.

Chapter 4

*"They abuse you. They silence you, and you love
them. They turn their backs. They say be quiet, and
you love them.
They don't protect you. They degrade you, and yet
still you love them."*

We are back in Texas. Mommy says I
don't get to go back to school here. This
state doesn't make kids go to school at
five years old like California. I miss going to
school, but at least I don't have to be with
kids that make fun of me, so it's okay. Our
house is real small. We kids have to share a
bedroom, with two sets of bunk beds in it.
Cossette, my little sister and I have to share
the bottom bunk of one. Sometimes she has
a nightmare and wets the bed. I get really
cold, so I sleep on the couch. Mommy says
it's not Cossette's fault she's still learning to
go to the potty. All I know is I get wet, and I
don't like it.

I must be having a dream about rain.
The window by our bed is open, and I'm
getting wet. My dream seems so real;
I can feel the dampness of the water on

my gown. I get up and go to the window. I push the stool my sisters use to get up on the top bunk under the window and close it. The next thing I remember is on the couch, and something was happening to me. No, I'm not on the couch I'm in Mommy and Daddy's' room. Someone is taking off my gown. It's my Daddy. No, I'm not dreaming. For some reason, I feel scared, and I have never been afraid of my Daddy.

I look up at him as my gown slides over my head and say, "Daddy did I get wet again?"

Now I can barely see Daddy's face. It's dark in the room. I feel him reach down to me. He picks me up, lays me on the bed and slips my underwear off.

Very Quietly he whispers, "Shhh, we don't want to wake no one up. Yes, your wet and cold you can sleep with me." But he didn't put a clean gown or panties on me. He just pulls the covers over both of us.

"Daddy, where's Mommy? I think I want I to go back to my bed." I whispered just as quietly.

"I said to be quiet and go to sleep!" He sounds mad.

I shut my eyes tight, so he would think I was asleep. Oh, I wish I had been dreaming. Then I could think of it as a nightmare and forget about it, cause what my Daddy did to me next was awful. I turn away from him. I feel him reach for me and turn me on to my back. At first, he was just playing with my hair and telling me what a good and brave little girl I am.

Rubbing my arm, he says, "Audrey, don't be afraid I love you and would never hurt you. Why are you shaking, just relax honey? I'm your Daddy it's okay.

While he was talking, Daddy had pulled the cover away and got on his knees' beside me. The moon was shining through the window now on my Daddy's face. He looks different. Not like my Daddy at all. *Mommy, get me. Please, Mommy, wake up and come to your bed wherever you are.*

I try to push away crying, "Daddy, I want Mommy. I'm scared. What are you doing?" He tells me to stop.

I'm scared. Why am I scared? My legs are shaking. I just want to run. I feel him put his hand over my mouth.

The next thing I remember is standing next to the bed and Daddy says I can go and get in my bed.

"Audrey, don't say anything about this. If you do, they will take you away, and you won't see any of us again. It will be our little secret, okay?" I nodded and grabbed my clothes.

Running into the living room, I stop when I reach the couch. I'm not going to sleep there; I'm too afraid. I stop because I found my Mommy. She was sleeping right here all along. I hesitate for a minute then run back and crawl into bed with my little sister. The bed feels even wetter, but I didn't care. I curled into a ball and started to cry quietly. I don't remember putting my dirty wet gown back on, but I had. I don't know what Daddy did to me, but it hurts really bad. It hurts to move my legs, especially at the top where I go potty. I think I wet my panties. After lying still for a very long time I realize I need to go potty, but I can't move. I'm afraid to close my eyes and go to sleep. For the first time, I'm afraid of my Daddy. *Daddy lied to me. He hurt me. He hurt me so bad.*

The sun finally is up. It's morning. I here Mommy go into the kitchen and turn on the water. She calls for Daddy to get up. Daddy is in the kitchen with Mommy, and they're talking. I can hear Mommy. She is angry with Daddy. I don't know why this scared me, but it did. My legs start shaking again.

Mommy burst into our bedroom and yells for us to get up.

"My God, it stinks in here." She says as she pulls the covers off of Cossette and me.

"Carmen, get up and change Cossette. Audrey, come with me." Shaking I put my feet on the ground to follow her and fall.

"What's the matter with you? Get up. You need a bath. Audrey, this isn't like you. You're usually the first one to come and complain when your little sister wets the bed. My God, you stink." She is saying this as she drags me to the bathroom where Carmen is running my bath.

I sit down on the toilet and look at the floor. Carmen turns to me and says, "Come on Audrey, let me help you get your gown off. Oh, Momma is right, you do stink." She looks at my face and says she sorry.

"It's okay I know it's not your fault. Come on let's get you into the water before Momma comes back. Momma's not in a good mood today, and she's late for work." Carmen starts to raise my gown, but I hold on to it.

"No, no let me. I can take my bath! I don't need your help." Carmen stood up and looked down at me.

Gasping for air, I say. "Really sister, I can do it. Go help clean Cossette up, okay?"

As she walks out the door, she says for me to hurry up or she will come back and help me. I slowly take off my gown and underwear. As I stepped into the tub, careful to hold on to the towel bar, Carmen walks back in saying.

"Sorry but Momma wants me to help you. Oh, my Gosh! Audrey, what happened? Did you hurt yourself? Audrey, there's blood right there."

I looked down where Brenda was looking and started to shake, "Oh, I think I must have hurt myself when I fell out of bed last night. I rolled the wrong way. I thought it was raining on me, and I was getting wet. I hurt my mouth too. See, I scraped it when I fell." *Please believe me, Carmen, I prayed. Oh please believe me.*

She leans over the tub; shaking her head and clicking her tongue like she is a Mommy, "Here let me help. There, now let's get your hair washed."

"Carmen, Don't tell Mommy okay? She'll just get mad at me, and I think she's mad enough today already." I keep peeking up at Carmen.

"It will be our secret. Just be more careful, okay?" Carmen say's, with a troubled look crossing her face. *She can't know what happened. Nobody can.*

I guess there are two kinds of secrets, one's that can hurt, and one's that are to protect you. I'm just not sure which is which.

Things seem to change after that, or maybe I did. Maybe I start noticing things that went on around me more. I know I become very quiet. I guess I thought if no one saw or heard me I will be okay. Mommy and Daddy are upset with each other more. The arguing is getting worse. A few months later during the night everything seems to fall apart.

Waking up from a deep sleep, I rub my eyes. I hear Mommy crying and yelling for us to get into the car, "C'mon hurry! Audrey, take your little sister Cossette, and put her in the back of the station wagon. No, no! Don't worry about shoes just go! Junior, go with them. Now!"

"Momma, what's wrong?" I grunt while trying to lift my sleeping little sister from the bed.

Momma's bottom lip is trembling when she speaks, "Carmen has to go to the hospital. No more questions, Audrey. Go!"

Walking into the living room, I see Daddy picking Carmen up from the couch.

Momma makes me jump when she screams, "Don't you touch her, Cameron. Put her down. Ceely, help your sister to the car."

Riding in the car sitting next to Carmen I could hear her whimper. I don't know what to say or do. I wish I knew what is wrong. Carmen doesn't look hurt. Looking down at her hands folded in her lap, I gasped, "Carmen what happened? You're bleeding." I saw blood on the hem of her dress, too.

She put her finger to her lips and shook her head. "I don't know. I just hurt, Audrey. Somehow I hurt myself down there. Please, leave me alone. I don't want to talk about it." Carmen leans over and lays her head in my lap.

Daddy stops the car in front of the hospital. Momma helps Carmen out. When I slide over to get out with them, she says for me to stay with Daddy. I don't remember leaving the hospital. I must have fallen asleep.

No one ever talked about it, again. I guess that's when I realized we were never supposed to talk about bad things that happen to us. I knew if we talked we would be separated. I didn't want to be taken away from my brother and sisters no matter how bad it got. Carmen, and I never talked about what happened to her or me. I think I knew Daddy had hurt both of us. I just blocked it out like it never happened, but Carmen isn't as lucky. I think Daddy hurts Carmen, now. She is quite and cries a lot, but I never ask her what's wrong. I don't want to know. Somehow I knew, if it wasn't said aloud, then it didn't happen.

Chapter 5

*"Her eyes are closed against the pain. The fields
are fresh with fallen rain. In her mind all is clean.
The beautiful rose holds all her dreams. Her smile
is bright with youthful faith. Tomorrow will be her
saving grace."*

I start to school today. Daddy is going
to drop us off our first day, but after that,
we have to walk. Carmen and Ceely
are complaining, but I think it will be fun.
They say it's too far, and they will have to
drag me with them. Oh well, they are the
big sisters, as they always like to remind
me. Oh yes, we moved. This house is
much bigger; even though it has only
two bedrooms, they are really big. We
won't be here long, though; Mommy is
pregnant again, and we will have to get
a place with more bedrooms. That's what
Grandmother says. I'm so glad to be going
to school; now I won't have to watch my
little brother and sister anymore. I only had
to watch them when Daddy works which
isn't very often, but I don't like doing it. I
always get afraid when we are left alone;

sometimes Carmen or Ceely have to stay home from school with us. Then sometimes Daddy will keep one of them home. I don't know why because he would be there. I remember they would cry and beg Mommy to let them go to school. She would tell them Daddy isn't feeling good, and he wants one of them to help with the kids. Mommy makes the one who hadn't missed as much school stay home. Usually, it is Carmen. Ceely got sick a lot with a cough, so Mommy didn't like her to miss too much school. I didn't like it cause Daddy always made us take a nap when one of them were home, but they got to stay up. That was the times I would notice Carmen crying. She woke me up sometimes after I had been asleep for a while, crawling in bed with me. I just thought she was upset not getting to go to school. I felt sad for her so I would hug her back.

It was different when Ceely stayed home. Many times when I would get up, she would be sitting on the couch, with her ankles crossed out in front of her. Her hands would be on her lap, balled in fists, just giving Daddy these mean looks. Daddy would be watching TV and smoking. Now and then he would give her some scary looks back, but Ceely never looked away. We thought Ceely was brave. One time she made Daddy so mad she had to lock herself in the bathroom. I woke up to her screaming and him beating on the bathroom door. I was so scared for Ceely. Ceely, stayed in there until Mommy got home. Daddy told Mommy what Ceely had done. When Ceely tried to tell Mommy that Daddy had scared her, Mommy said for her to be quiet. She told Ceely she was always doing things to make her Daddy mad, and she wanted it to stop now. She didn't ever want to have to come home to something like this again. I tried to tell Mommy too, that it wasn't Ceely's fault. I thought Daddy wanted to hurt Ceely, but Momma wouldn't listen to me either. She would get sent to our room. Ceely said she didn't mind; she would rather be by herself. She would never cry. Ceely said she would never let them see her cry. They would not make her cry, and she didn't. I can't ever remember seeing her cry. I so looked up to Ceely. I wished I could be as brave as she is.

After that Momma and Daddy sent Ceely to stay with Maw Maw and Paw Paw on the weekends. That's my Daddy's parents. Carmen and I took turns staying the weekends with Grandmother and Granddaddy. That's my Momma's parents. That was fine with me. I will get to see my two best friends Jasmin and Franny. They live next door and across the street from my grandparents. We never get to have many friends and the ones we have are never allowed to come to our house. Momma said she had enough kids, but that was okay with us. We didn't want our friends to come over, either.

One good thing about my Grandparents, they never moved. They have lived in Oak Cliff since my Momma was a little girl, so even though we never stay long anywhere, I always have friends that live near my Grandmothers' house. I love going to stay with my Grandparents. It's always clean. Grandmother always has to have her house spotless, as she calls it. She also will make me whatever I want to eat. I used to giggle at Junior, my little brother because all he ever wants is *Cereal*. You can bet my Grandparents made sure they had plenty for him, too. I guess Carmen and I stay the most with Grandmother and Granddaddy. The other kids didn't like to stay because our Grandmother has this thing about making us take a bath every time we come in from outside. Sometimes you get three baths a day. She always buys us new clothes, too. She says the ones we had made us look like *rag-a-muffins*, and she isn't going to be seen out in public with us like that. She is always muttering under her breath how she hadn't raised our Mother like that. Grandmother would shake her head and wonder out loud, *where she went wrong.*

My grandmothers' house is where I can just be myself. I don't have to share a bed with four other kids. I know I am safe there. Granddaddy could be grouchy sometimes, but I know he loves me. I will sit forever in their backyard. Granddaddy had a beautiful yard. Daddy said he took pride in everything he grew. Momma said he used to work for a Nursery. I thought that was funny. Nurseries were for babies, but Momma said that's what you call where they grow plants and flowers too. Well, all I know is, his grass was the greenest and thickest I have ever seen, and there are every plant and flower you can imagine. There is a bug called *Chiggers*. Grandmother says they love to bite little kids, so she always was powdering us with this stuff called *sulfur* to keep them away.

That's also why we had to take a bath every time we came in from outside. *I told you, my Grandmother likes everything clean all the time.*

My friend Jasmin and I used to play out in the back yard for hours. We would pretend we were butterflies and run through Granddaddy's garden. We are in awe of all the colors and smells. He has pear and fig trees, too. It is like paradise for two little girls. Sometimes we play like we are Mommies. Jasmin will be a Mommy. I'm always a Grandmother. Today is no different when she come over to play.

She says that is stupid, "Audrey, everyone knows that Grandmothers' don't have babies. They're too old."

She hurt me so I tell her, "Well, this one does. Sometimes kids can live with their grandparents." She shrugged her shoulders and said to be whoever I want to be.

Jasmin and I are like sisters. No, it was better than that; we are like twins. We share everything. Well, almost everything. I never share secrets about my family, with her. She likes my Daddy. She said he is fun to be around, but all kids say that about my Daddy. My cousins think we are lucky to have a Daddy that will joke and play games with you, but they don't know him like we do. Daddy is fun most of the time; just sometimes I feel like he isn't my Daddy at all. I always know my Grandparents, though. I know I have somewhere to go and be happy all the time, until I would have to go home, again. Carmen always cries and throws a fit when Momma comes to get her. She even sass's Momma and will call her names; which is something we are not supposed to do. Momma would threaten Carmen that she can't come back if she doesn't stop. Grandmother would cry because she thought Momma meant it. I knew better. Momma always let her come back. I knew Momma needed our Grandmother. I know how much Grandmother helps Momma with us kids. When you're a little kid grown-ups, tend to forget you're there. They say and do things they think you won't understand, but I do watch, and I listen. I know how important my Grandmother is to us kids, and I love her for it.

For me, my Granddaddy's, *field of flowers*, is my safe place to go when I am sad or just want to block out something bad that is happening at home. In my mind I go there, *a beautiful butterfly with multicolor wings, dancing among the flowers.* You would never know their house is in a big city covered with concrete. Grandmother and Granddaddy's house is my safe place. Somehow I know to keep it separate from my home with Momma and Daddy. I know that this is what I want when I grow up. I want a place like this for my babies; somewhere they can play and feel safe, and to know they are loved. I know I can never tell grandmother and granddaddy, about the things that go on at home with Mommy and Daddy. I don't want to be taken away from my family. *My family secrets will be locked in my mind by a field of flowers surrounded by concrete.*

Chapter 6

"The innocent is the last to be heard.
They lower their heads. They walk away. They hide
their tears, and nothing is said."

Our weekend visits with Grandmother and Granddaddy lasted a few months. That is until today. Momma went to the hospital to have my little brother, Craig. Daddy said Ceely and Carmen would have to stay home to help take care of him.

"Audrey, you and Cossette will continue to stay with your grandparents on the weekends for awhile."

I guess two fewer kids in the house made it easier. Momma told Daddy he had to find a job. She couldn't go back to work until Craig was a little older, so Daddy called my uncle Adam that night and went to work with him. Things went smooth for the next month, but then I guess Momma was tired of staying home because she went back to work. She got a job working at night, so she or Daddy could always be home for Craig.

The next few years were okay. Oh, Momma and Daddy still fought a lot, but Carmen, Ceely and me got to go to school more. I loved my first, second and third grade at Lisbon Elementary School. There were those kids that had to be mean, but I learned how to stay clear of them most of the time. I had nice teachers, too; except for my third-grade teacher, Mrs. Sneed. My first, second and third grades were the longest we stayed in one school district. By the beginning of this year, my fourth grade, we were moving again.

This school was different. It's not the kids that are bad it's the teacher. I hate my fourth-grade teacher. I know Daddy said we are not supposed to hate anyone, but that's the only word I can think to use. She isn't just mean to me, but to a lot of kids. She seems always to want to embarrass us. It's like it makes her happy. I have long hair, and today during our free period a girl in my class, Sheila, was brushing my hair and braiding it. Our teacher walks up and takes her brush and throws it in the garbage. She makes us hold our arms straight out. She then grabbed our hand and turned it, so the palm was up. Before we know what is happening, she raises the ruler and hits us across our palms. That is a sting I will never forget. My hand burns and there are small red lines puffing up on it. I try to make a fist, but it hurts too bad. The teacher took me by the arm and said to follow her. Standing in front of the class she gave us the worst punishment we could have gotten, she told everyone never to do what we had been doing.

She began by saying, "Class I want you all to look up here at these two girls. Hear me and hear me good. A black child is never to use a comb or brush on a white child's hair that has been used on their hair first or the same punishment will befall you!" She then hit our other hand. For good measure, she says and then places Sheila and me in opposite corners of the room until the class is over.

I have never been hit like that before, and it hurt so bad, but I wasn't going to cry. President Kennedy talks about the word prejudice and what it means to our Nation. I saw how ugly it could be that day.

I walked over to Sheila and said, "I'm so sorry for getting us in trouble, Sheila. Listen we can still be friends just not at school, I guess."

"Just stay away from me. That's what this is all about, Audrey. We can't be friends; I know you're not that stupid." She turned and walked away with her friends.

It was worse when I got home. The teacher had sent a note home to my Mother. When Momma read it, she was mad, at me!

"Don't you ever let that happen again. Oh my God! You probably have *head lice* now. Come here let me check your hair." She was yelling like I had committed the worst crime in the world.

"Momma, she hit us with a ruler and then embarrassed us in front of the whole class. What she said wasn't fair. Ouch!" It felt like she was pulling my hair out.

"Well, everybody knows that *Coloreds* have *head lice*. What were you thinking? No, she shouldn't have hit you. I will talk to her about that, but that girl should have known better." She said this as she dragged me to the kitchen to wash my hair.

"Momma, are you saying white people don't get bugs in their hair? Why should she have known better? I didn't, and we are the same age. Momma, she's my friend. Her name is Sheila, and it was wrong what happened to her, too. Ouch!" I said this just as Momma hit me on the top of my head and told me to be still.

"Well, you better make new friends and don't think you're going to start bringing any *Colored* friends home with you, either. That's just the way it is Audrey. Whites stay with whites and *Coloreds* stay with their kind." She said this with contempt in her voice. At that moment I didn't like my Momma very much.

"Momma, we don't get to bring friends home, no matter what color they are. Also, her skin is black, and my skin is white so doesn't that make us all *Colored people*? Why does everyone call them *Coloreds*? You make being *Colored* sound like a bad thing." I am only nine, and I never talk back to Momma, but this didn't seem right to me.

"Audrey Rose, I am only going to say this once. I am your mother, and you do as I say and don't question me. Do you understand?" She was glaring down at me.

I knew I was real close to getting a *switch* on my legs, so I said yes. Momma always made sure she had fresh small limbs cut from a tree to keep near her in case we got out of hand. We had to cut six, one for each of us. The thought of that thin *switch*-hitting my leg brought tears to my eyes, so I lowered my eyes and told her I was sorry.

"That's better. I will talk to your teacher tomorrow. Go clean the bathroom and then get your homework done," That's how it always goes with my Momma. She was right, and you never ask why.

The next day at school my teacher called me to her desk. She said my Mother had come to see her that morning. She said she was not afraid of my mother. *The Board Of Education* has rules if the students act up they are to be punished as the school sees fit. If I did something foolish like that again, I would get the same punishment. She lowers her voice and squints her eyes. She said she would be watching me, so I better be careful, and then she sent Sheila and me to the Nurses office to get our hair checked for *Lice*. My Momma told her she would hold the school responsible if I brought *Head Lice* home to the rest of her kids. Needless to say, I will never tell Momma anything that goes on in class again. The teacher made a new seating chart for the whole class, too. She said, so Sheila and I wouldn't be tempted again, all the *Colored* students were to sit in the desks at the back of the room. She made sure the class knew that it was my fault. Sheila never talked to me again, and I didn't blame her. Even though I had to suffer through all that, I knew I still had it better than Sheila, because my skin is white. By the way, neither Maggie nor I had *Lice.*

Not long after that, there was a contest in our school for *fire prevention month.* The girl and boy who went to the most houses and did a fire inspection would win a bicycle. They gave us a packet of papers called *Fire Prevention Checklists* and we were supposed to go inside and make sure each house we inspected followed the rules on safety for fire prevention in the home. Then we had to get the homeowner to sign and date it. I knew all about what a fire could do to you, so I worked hard to get the most inspections done. Plus, I wanted the bicycle. I always tried to take one of my brothers or sisters with me, usually Junior. Sometimes I have to go by myself. When the contest is finally over, and the lists are counted. I hadn't won the bicycle, but I had *won second place.* The Principal said I didn't win the bike but my whole family, and I was going to get to go to the State Fair of Texas free. I was also going to get a badge from the *Fire Marshall*, and I would be on TV with the rest of the kids that won in the school district. I was so excited; my legs shook as I walked across the stage to get my *certificate and badge*.

When I went back to school on Monday, the Principal came to our class and said we would get to have candy and play all day. He said a boy and I won for our homeroom class. I was so excited, but that didn't last long. Our teacher said I probably cheated and got my family to sign all those lists. She said there was no way I could have done that alone. I wanted to cry, but I didn't. She only let me have half a free day, and I didn't get any candy. That's okay, though, I knew, and my classmates knew I had won. I couldn't understand why she hated me so much. What did I do to make her not like me? I tried to do all my work, and no matter how well I did, it wasn't good enough. I tried to stay quiet and not be noticed by her, but she always seemed to find something wrong with my work or me. I got where I didn't want to go to school. I begged Momma to put me in another class, and she tried, but they said there was no room. For once, I wished we would move.

The other day when I got home from school, no one was there. Carmen and Ceely arrived later. I asked them where Mommy and Daddy were? They didn't know either. We had just finished our chores and homework when Momma and Daddy walk in together. I knew something wrong. Momma put Craig to bed, and Daddy sat down in a chair across from the couch. Junior and Cossette looked scared or was it sad. They stood next to Daddy looking up at him. He was staring off into space. Momma came back and told us to get ready for bed, though it was still early.

"Momma it's too early to go to bed. Can't we just finish watching this TV show first? Where have Y'all been? We were getting worried," Ceely asked the question Carmen, and I was afraid to.

"I said get ready for bed. Don't worry about your baths, just go to bed." Momma was looking at Daddy as she said this. Daddy looked up and yelled at Momma.

"No Carly! They need to know. For once, treat them like their part of this family. Your Paw Paw died today! Do you hear me! My dad died today! He won't be here anymore! You will never see him again!

None of us will!" Daddy's eyes were wide, and he was screaming at us.

"Cameron, stop it! I know you're hurting, but you're scaring them. Carmen, take the kids to bed." Daddy dropped to his knees in front of Momma. He was crying so hard his shoulders were shaking.

I had never seen my Daddy cry before; it scares me. My heart is breaking for him. Then his words sank in; my Paw Paw is dead. My sweet, sweet Paw Paw. He was the *Ice Cream Man*. I will always remember him in his truck with the music-playing children's nursery rhymes. He loved children. I will miss him so much, but I was more afraid of how Daddy was taking this. I had never seen my Daddy fall apart, as Momma called it. I knew our lives would never be the same. Who could have thought it would get any worse. As I turn to go to bed Daddy is still crying, and Momma tells him he had to get control of himself. I think for the first time my Momma was afraid. She calls one of my uncles to help her.

When my Uncle arrives, I was in the bedroom with the rest of the kids. No one realized how bad Ceely would take this. We all forgot how close she was to Maw Maw and Paw Paw. She was lying on the bed crying. Carmen was trying to comfort her. I didn't know what to do. Ceely doesn't cry. I just didn't know what to do; awhile-later Momma came in to talk to Ceely. She said Paw Paw had been sick. It was his heart. Ceely said it wasn't fair.

"Why did God have to take him? Why did he have to die? He never hurt anyone? Paw Paw was all I had. He's the only one who ever understood me! He loved me!" I could tell Momma didn't know what to say. Momma didn't care for Maw Maw much, but she liked Paw Paw. She just kept agreeing with Donna and finally told her to go to sleep, but she didn't. Ceely cried all night.

After the funeral we all went to Maw Maws' and then came home. It was sad. That was the first dead person I had ever seen. My Daddy picked me up and made me kiss Paw Paw goodbye. It's awful; he is so cold. I will never forget it. I tried to tell Daddy I didn't want to, but he got mad and made me. From that day on our lives turned into a living nightmare, Daddy only got worse. Tonight it got bad. He was ranting and raving at Momma and us kids. Momma finally got Uncle Eli and Uncle

Adam to come over. They told Daddy he better get a grip on things, or he would have to be taken out of the house. Daddy told them he would be okay.

Momma went back to work the next day, but she told me to stay home with Daddy to help with Randy. I think Momma was afraid to leave Daddy alone with him. Everyone else went back to school. That was okay with me. I hated my school. Everything was okay that day. Daddy and I talked a lot. He told me about growing up with his parents and five brothers. He told me he had had a little sister, but she died when she was real little. Daddy said that it hurt Maw Maw and Paw Paw so much that Maw Maw didn't talk to anyone for days.

"I think that she blamed my Dad because they didn't have the money to get her help from a doctor. I feel really bad now cause, after losing your Paw Paw I know how she felt, but at the time I was mad at her. She ignored my brothers and me as if we had something to do with our sister dying." Daddy stopped talking. I knew he was thinking about the little sister he lost.

Daddy startled me. He grabbed my hands and said, "Audrey, when someone hurts you, you must always think of what they are going through before you get angry at them. Never say something you wish you could take back and if you do, don't wait to tell them you're sorry. You may not get another chance with them." Daddy had tears in his eyes again. I understood what he was saying. I wish I could take his pain away.

The next day Momma told Carmen to stay home, but after Momma had gone to work, I told Carmen I would. She looks relieved. She likes her school. It didn't take me long to realize I had made a big mistake staying home. I had just laid Craig down for his nap when Daddy yelled for me. He said for me to come into the dining room. When I got there, he had the Bible lying on the table. For the next four hours, I was schooled on the Bible, and how evil I was because I was a girl.

"Most women in the Bible are *Whores* you know! They're the root of all that's evil. God made men superior. Women were made to serve men. Audrey, do you understand what I'm telling you?" I understood, but I didn't believe him. Of course, I wasn't going to tell him that. I was scared, and this wasn't my Daddy talking.

"Yes, Daddy I understand. It was because Eve ate that apple, huh," my voice was trembling as I said this.

"Daddy I need to go get Craig out of bed and feed him," I said this hoping he would remember why I was home from school. Nope didn't work. He wouldn't even let me get up to feed Craig.

Craig must have crawled out of his crib. He was too big for a crib, but that was the only bed we had for him. He came up quietly next to my chair and looks up at me without saying a word. I finally whispered to Craig, during one of Daddy's outbursts, to get a chair and get himself some dry cereal. Craig was almost three. His Birthday was next month, March.

Right before it was time for Momma to get home Daddy starts acting like his old self. Like the day never happened. I tell Momma I had stayed home again and how Daddy was acting. She didn't like that I stayed home and said I had to go to school tomorrow. I said I would. When she asked daddy about what he had put me through; he said I was lying. He said I made it up so she wouldn't be mad that I stayed out of school. Momma never said, but I think she believed him. Carmen had to stay home the next day. I felt bad for Carmen, but I was glad to be going to school. Ceely and I were almost out the door when Daddy called us back in. He told Carmen she was going to school, and I was staying home with Craig today.

"But Daddy, Momma said I had to go to school. Daddy, I have missed too much already." I did not want to stay home. I knew Daddy was mad at me.

"Carmen, get your stuff. I will take y'all to school and then I am going to work. I don't care what your mother said. You will listen to me. Didn't you hear anything I said yesterday, Audrey?" This *man* is not my Daddy; he had a look in his eye's I had never seen before. His voice was even different. It was evil.

"It's okay Carmen; I'll stay home. Get your stuff. Yes, Daddy, I heard you yesterday, I know you're the boss," I said this with as much of a grown-up voice as I could for nine and a half years old.

For some reason, I knew I had to appear strong to him. I had to be somebody I wasn't. I just didn't know who that was. Carmen gave me a shaky smile. She didn't want to leave me, but I felt safe since Daddy was going to work. I had just laid

Craig down for his nap when I heard the front door open. I thought Momma had come home for lunch like she sometimes did, but it wasn't Momma it was a Daddy. He walks in without looking at me and goes straight to his bedroom. When he came out, he had his Bible. He grabbed me and sat me down on the couch.

"Now I am going to teach you what happens to liars. The Bible says you are a sinner. Do you know what happens to sinners? No, of course, you don't, because you are one! Well, the Bible says for you to obey your Mother and Father!" With that, he grabs my arm again and drags me to his bedroom and slams the door.

I'm so scared, but I'm more afraid that he will wake up Craig. For some reason I knew; Craig had to stay asleep for him to be safe. Hopefully, Daddy will forget he is here. What happened next was the most horrifying thing any nine-year-old should have to go through at the hands of her Father. As he took off my clothes, I was screaming, but nothing was coming out of my throat. It was all in my head. The sound I heard was a little girl screaming, not me. I stood there shivering in nothing but my underwear staring at him. He threw me on the bed and took off his belt. I thought he was going to hit me, but he didn't. Oh, I wish he had. I could have taken that. Daddy did the most unspeakable things to me all the while quoting, *The Bible*. Calling me a sinner and a whore. I kept trying to get away.

"Daddy, please let me go. I promise I'll be good. Daddy get your Bible and shows me again what I did wrong. I promise to learn it this time. Daddy, I'll never tell Momma again. Please, Daddy just let me go!" I was crying so hard I could barely understand what I was saying, but I knew I had to talk him out of this.

"You're right. You won't tell your Momma again, cause if you do they will take you away. You and your brothers and sisters will never see each other again. Do you understand me?" He didn't wait for an answer.

I made my mind go blank. I didn't understand what he was doing. All I knew is that I wanted it to be over.

I saw the beautiful butterfly, gently floating on the wind. I saw the little girl. She looked to be about five years old. She was in my Granddaddy's field of flowers. I knew I was safe here, with her. No one, not even

Daddy could touch me here. I heard the birds singing. I reached out and picked a fragrant flower. I brought it to my nose. There it was, just what I had been waiting for, the smell of Roses and Honey Suckle. I followed the little girl to the house. I was safe in my grandmothers' kitchen. She was holding me. Humming a gentle tune in my ear. Telling me, she loved me and would always be there for me. The little girl was dancing around us singing. The back door to the kitchen opened and then slammed shut. Suddenly I was jolted back to my Momma and Daddy's bedroom.

It was over. Daddy was leaving. I was afraid to move. I waited until I was sure I was alone. I slowly got up and crawled into the bedroom I shared with my sisters. I took the blanket off our bed. I wrapped myself in it. It hurt so much to move. I checked on Craig and then peeked out the front door. He was gone. The driveway was empty. I locked the screen and closed the front door he had left opened. I went into the bathroom, ran some hot water, and got in. I don't know how long I had been in the tub. When I heard my brother and sisters' come home. The next thing I know Carmen is calling my name, and banging on the bathroom door. I tell her I will be out in a minute. Ceely is sitting on the couch playing with Craig. Cossette and Junior are watching TV. Carmen is getting dinner ready. Daddy and Momma are nowhere in sight. I go into the kitchen to help Brenda. She takes one look at me, and I start to cry. She hugs me and tells me to go lay down until Momma got home.

"What did Daddy do?" She says this so matter-of-factly. I just shake my head. I can't tell her. "That's okay, it wouldn't do any good to tell me anyway, but at least tell Momma."

"I don't know if I can, Carmen. I'm afraid she won't believe me." I mutter as if mentioning it would make it true.

I turn and walk out of the kitchen. I look into the living room; everything looks normal. I could never live apart from my brothers and sisters. I slowly walk to our bedroom. Every step seems heavy as if I'm walking in water. I lay down on the bed lost in thought. Carmen yells, dinner, is ready. I say I don't want any. She says I need to eat, but she understands. A little later Momma came home. Daddy still isn't home yet. I hear Brenda talking to Momma in a soft voice. Momma walks into my room.

"Audrey, what's wrong? What happened today? Brenda says, your Dad kept you out of school, again. What did he do? Did he make you read the Bible again?" Oh, Momma, I thought to myself. I wish that's all he made me do. I could tell she doesn't want to know. She wants me to say nothing happened, cause that's how Momma is.

I started to cry. I always have to cry when I'm upset. Why can't I be as strong as Ceely? I don't tell Momma everything, just that he touched me in places a Daddy shouldn't touch his daughter. I tell her he is *crazy!*

"He called me a liar and a *sinner.* He said I was a *Whore.* Momma, what does that mean? He was mad at me for telling you how he acted yesterday. What's wrong with him?" I'm crying anymore. I'm mad.

"Audrey, all I can tell you is that your Daddy is sick. He hasn't been the same since your Paw Paw died. I am going to get him help if he will let me. You girls are going to have to stop upsetting your Dad." She pats me on the head as if I'm a little puppy. She told me to eat, and not to worry she will take care of things. No hugs, no I love you, *just I will take care of things.* At the door she turns and in a light voice, she says.

"Oh, and Audrey don't mention this to anyone. They won't understand your Dad like we do." I was looking at her as if she had gone crazy, too.

"Believe me when I say this. They will take you kids away from me. Is that what you want." I shake my head no.

"Okay then, I will take care of this I promise." I didn't tell her that Daddy was sick way before Paw Paw died. I just didn't know then, what sick meant.

When Daddy came home, he acted as if nothing happened. He was the old Daddy, again. I went back to school the next day. Daddy didn't try to stop me. He said I had better find something I liked about that school because I couldn't miss any more days. I know I must had looked at him like he had grown horns are something. He said he understood how I felt, but we all have to do things we don't like, and then he turned to Carmen.

"Carmen, you will be home today. Ceely, it's your turn tomorrow." Nothing else was said.

On the way to school, I thought about if Momma had talked to Daddy; either

Momma didn't say anything to him, or she believed whatever lie he told her. I also knew now; my Daddy could tell my Momma a lie, and she would believe him over us kids. I guess that would be right; after all, *you don't expect an adult to lie to you.* Maybe it was my fault. Maybe Momma was right. I will never do anything to upset Daddy again. I vow from this day on I will be as quiet as a mouse. No one will know I'm around. I will do whatever Daddy and Momma asked me to do without an argument. I don't want ever to have to go through that again. I don't think I would want to live anymore. I said a silent prayer to Jesus to protect me.

When I got to my classroom and gave the teacher my absent excuse note. She was still upset with me, she said she didn't care that my Paw Paw had died.

"No one misses that many days of school because someone died. It will take you forever to catch up, and I doubt if you can," she said this with a snorting sound.

"People like your parents don't put much value on an education. That's why they're poor. Your kind doesn't care. They think everything should be handed to them. Everyone should feel sorry for them." I just handed her my note and went to my desk. She was still scolding me as I walked off.

All the kids were staring at me. I didn't care. I didn't care what my teacher said to me. The things my teacher said couldn't hurt me anymore. My Momma and Daddy hurt me more than anything or anyone else could.

At nine years old I know I have to protect myself and my brothers and sisters. We have no one. Our Grandparents can't help us. They don't want to lose us either. My Aunts and Uncles are too busy with their kids. We don't have close friends; we aren't allowed too. Our teachers and neighbors, well what could they do; when we are too afraid to talk to anyone about it, besides what good would it do to tell them. They will just have us taken away. It really wouldn't be hard for an adult to tell there was something wrong at our house, but I guess they are too busy. Maybe they thought it isn't any of their business and just don't want to get involved.

No, all we have is each other, maybe it's not the right thing to do, but I will keep quiet. I will be the best little girl I can be, and when I have to, I will go to my field of flowers.

Chapter 7

"They live in darkness; for they will never know. The little girl who loves them so.
They live in darkness; for now, they will never know."

Everything in my world was okay for a while. Not in our house, but in my world. Daddy didn't make me stay home again. It was as if he didn't notice I was home at all. I went to school. I came home and did my chores. I went to my room and worked on homework or read a book. I came out to eat dinner. Cleaned the kitchen when it was my turn. I would then go back to my room and stay until it was time to go to bed. If I were told to watch TV with the family, or go outside and play, I did. I would help get my little brother and sister ready for school. I would have stood on my head if they had asked me too. I did whatever I had to do to keep myself safe, and it worked for a while. Then it all came crumbling down. One morning in April, two months almost to the day my Paw Paw died. Momma got up to go to work. Daddy had quit working, again by then. It was a morning like any other;

until we were about to leave. Momma had opened the door to leave, but Daddy told her no.

"Carly! Shut the door and come sit down. You too kids, get in here at the table, now! Carly, I said now!" He had that look in his eyes again. Momma must have seen it too because she told us to sit down

"Cameron, what are you doing? I'll be late for work. The kids have to go to school. Are you okay? Do you want me to call one of your brothers?"

That just made Daddy mad. He banged his fist down on the table and told Momma to shut up. He walked up behind her and grabbed a hand full of her hair.

"Boy's you go in your room and play. Carmen, go and get my Bible. Now! I know I have taught you, girls, this lesson, but your momma needs to hear it." He was glaring at Momma as he said this.

Carmen ran into their bedroom and got the Bible. Daddy smiled at her and said she was his best daughter and kissed her on her cheek. Carmen kind of pulled away, but he didn't notice. When he started talking about how the women were in the Bible, and what their place was in the home, I started shaking. I wanted to run. I just wanted to run, but I didn't. I looked at my little sister, Cossette. She had tears in her eyes because Daddy was yelling. He was getting right in Mommas' face like she couldn't hear him or something, this went on for hours. At first, Momma tried to talk to him, but he just got more upset, so she quit. Finally, Daddy told Ceely and me to make something for lunch. We couldn't get up fast enough. When we got to the kitchen, Ceely said we should try to sneak out and get help. I was too scared.

"Audrey, one of us has to go get help. I would, but Momma might need me. I'm bigger than you. Don't cry; that's not going to help anything." As she talked, she was looking out the window on the door.

"Ceely, he would kill us if we do that. You don't know. You just don't know how mean he can be, Ceely. It's better if we're all here." I could tell by the look on her face she was getting upset with me.

"Yes Audrey, I do know how mean Daddy can be. That's why one of us has to go for..." Donna must have noticed the look on my face.

About the time she spun around Daddy grabbed her arm, "I said to make lunch. Come on get back in here. Where's

Carmen, Carly? Carmen get in here, now! Sit down at the table, all of you." Daddy made Ceely sit right next to him.

He still had a hold of her arm. Ceely jerked it away. She gave him a look that dared him to hit her. Daddy just laughed and walked away.

"Carly, you better get control of your girls. No one is going to leave this house until I say so! Is that understood?" we all nodded. Cossette was sniffling. I just wanted to hold her.

"Now you two get back to the kitchen and get some food in here. If anyone tries to leave that will be the last thing you do. Don't make me hurt any of y'all. Is that clear?"

Trying to sound brave I say, "Yes Sir, we understand. Come on Ceely let's finish." We went back into the kitchen and in silence made lunch.

Daddy kept us at the table until it got dark. He had unplugged the TV and pulled the phone out the wall. Carmen had made Dinner. He wasn't going to let Momma leave his sight. After dinner, he told us to go to bed and to remember what he had said about leaving. When we got to the bedroom, Ceely went right to the window.

She tried to open it but then realized Daddy had nailed it shut.

"What are we going to do? I wonder how long he thinks he can keep us locked up?" Ceely sounded mad.

"I don't know Ceely, but we have to do what he says. Momma says he sick. Maybe it will be alright in the morning." Carmen says this sounding like, *she didn't even believe what she was saying.*

We all climbed into bed and held each other. All I can think is I hope we don't have to miss a lot of school. My teacher will never believe this, or she probably just wouldn't care. Oh, why does Daddy have to be this way?

Daddy, kept us locked in the house for almost three weeks. There would be days where we didn't get to eat. Daddy, made us listen to him read the Bible every day for hours. Some days we only got bread and water. Grandmother and Granddaddy came by once, but we had to act like everything was all right. Daddy threatened to hurt them if we didn't. Finally, Momma talked Daddy into letting her and Brenda go to the store. She said the little ones would die without food much longer. We were completely out of food and Daddy needed cigarettes. We had been living on red beans, cornbread, and tea. I was so afraid while they were gone, and it was taking them too long.

Something strange happened to Daddy while they were gone, though. He told us to go outside and play. He said since Momma decided not to send us to school we might as well have fun. Ceely and I were trying to figure out how to get the little ones out the backdoor and over the fence when we heard Momma come back. We walked back into the house just as two of our Uncles came in. Daddy was sitting on the couch. The TV was plugged back in, and he was acting like nothing was wrong.

My Uncle Adam says, "Cameron you need to get up, change clothes and go take a bath. No, don't say a word. You need help. Eli and I are going to get you to a doctor." Uncle Adam gave Daddy a look of disgust; although both of Daddy's brothers looked sad, too.

I know they loved my Daddy. We all did, no matter what he had done. We all knew Daddy was sick in his mind and his heart. When Daddy was ready to leave, he just asked Momma if she got him some cigarettes. She gave them to him, and he left with my Uncles.

Daddy stayed in Parkland Hospital for two weeks on their mental ward and then he went home with my Uncle, Adam. After a couple more weeks' Momma let Daddy come home. She said the doctor had him on medication and that he would be fine now. Uncle Adam had got Daddy a job. Carmen, Ceely and I were afraid. We didn't want him to come home yet. The little ones did, they missed our Daddy. Momma was right, though; Daddy seemed different. It is like we have our old Daddy back. He went to work every day. When he came home, he brought us candy.

Every Friday he would give us an allowance, and take us to the Five and Dime. We are happy. We are a family again, even though Momma and Daddy still fought. They would hit each other sometimes. Daddy always would put us in a room and tell us not to come out, but we could still hear them. Carmen always jumped out the window and ran to grandmothers' house to get help. No matter how far we lived from them, she still went. The police would come, and Daddy would beg Momma not to send him to

Jail. He would promise not to beat her any more, so she would let him stay. Everything would be okay for a few days then it would start all over again. Many times we begged Momma not to make Daddy mad, but she never listened to us. A couple of times she had the police take Daddy away, but he would be back by the next day.

By the time I started fifth grade we had moved back into Lisbon Elementary school district, this was fine with me I loved going to Lisbon. I have friends here. Of course, it was embarrassing, though. The kids were making fun of me for moving around all the time. It was also my favorite time of the year. Thanksgiving was almost here. The Holidays are always the happiest around our house. We have a tradition of putting up the Christmas tree on Thanksgiving Day. Daddy passed that tradition on to us. He said Paw Paw would cut down a tree on Thanksgiving, and they would decorate it after dinner, so that's what we do now. Daddy makes all our Holidays fun. He helps us make all the ornaments for the tree. He says homemade things come from the heart. They mean so much more than store bought. I knew that was true. We kids love the time we spent making ornaments together; when I think of one of my most happy memories, this is it. I also know we can't afford store bought, and that is okay too. No matter what Holiday it is Daddy does something special for us, kids. I can't remember him and Momma ever fighting on a Holiday.

Every year on Thanksgiving we always go to our Grandmother and Granddaddy's house. This year was no different. The women always cook. The men sit outside and talk. I think grandmother runs them outside because they have to smoke those nasty cigarettes, as she calls them. The kids, well we just play. We get to do what kids do best. On Christmas Eve we go to Grandmothers and open presents from her and Granddaddy. It's always the same thing, Pajamas. That's okay, though; we look forward to getting them. It wouldn't be Christmas without our new *Pj's*. Once we get home, we gather around the television to watch the radar on the news channel to see where *Santa* is. After that, it is off to bed so Daddy can read, *The Night Before Christmas.*" It never fails just as we are falling to sleep we hear, *Santa's bells* on his sleigh jingling. The next morning bright and early we get Momma and

Daddy up so we can open our presents. We usually only have one big present that Santa leaves and a couple of small ones from Momma and Daddy to open. Santa doesn't wrap his present. Then we go back to our grandparents for Christmas dinner. These are good *memories* I will carry with me always.

This holiday season would be different. On this night, November the 15th, 1963 Daddy got sick, again. It's his first Holiday season without Paw Paw. We were all in bed anticipating the holidays. Daddy had talked to us about getting the tree on Thanksgiving, and where we were going to put it. Momma's screams woke me up. I heard her keep saying Cameron, why. Cameron, why did you do this again? I turned over to wake Carmen and Ceely up, but Carmen wasn't there. Ceely and I ran into the living room and found Carmen sitting on the couch crying. Then we heard Daddy hit Momma. We grabbed Carmen and ran back into the bedroom. I don't know how long we stayed there listening to Daddy and Momma fight and argue. Daddy kept saying he wouldn't go back to Jail, or the Hospital. Momma said that's where he belonged, and after tonight that's where he was going. I don't know why Momma kept saying those things to him. It only made him madder at her. That's when we heard Momma scream for someone to help her. Carmen jumped out the window and went to grandmothers' for help. Thankfully we didn't live that far away. Grandmother sent the police. Momma told the police that Daddy was acting crazy and violent. She wants Daddy taken to a place called Terrell Hospital. They said they would send a car for him.

When the white and black car pulls up, two policemen get out. Momma sent us to her bedroom and told us to stay there and don't look out the window. Everything seems quite in the living room until we hear the front door open.

Daddy yells, "Boy's look at what your Mother is doing to me. I want you to see it with your own eyes," as he made the men drag him from the house.

"Do you see what those *whore's* in there are doing to me? Yes, your mother and sisters are having me put away. Don't trust them ever. They're liars and sinners. *God* put them here to serve you. You are the men of the house now. Take care of them until I come back."

The policemen were having a hard time getting Daddy into the car. I saw one of them take something out of the back of his pants. They throw my Daddy on the ground chaining his hands together. Then they forced Daddy into the back of the police car. I went to help Ceely pull the boy's away from the window. They were both crying for Momma not to do this to our Daddy. It was breaking my heart. When I finally was able to pull Craig over to Mommas' bed, I then notice Cossette. She is curled in a ball at the foot of the bed. I pull her up to where Craig and I were so that I could hold her too. Her little body was shaking, and I noticed her gown was soaking wet.

Oh, how could Momma and Daddy do this? Can't they see what they're putting us kids through? Do they even care? Ceely was still standing at the window holding onto Junior. They both were staring out the window. Their eyes look as if they are vacant; as if they are in a trance. People always commented on how all six of kids had the prettiest eyes; blue and our dark hair made them stand out even more. Wonder what they will think now. I wonder if anyone will notice the pain behind them. Probably not, no one cares.

The next day Momma told me she had to go to court to have my Daddy committed.

"Audrey, I want you to go with me."

"Do I have too, Momma?" My voice was shaking.

No, but I don't want to go alone." She sounds worried.

"Momma, will Daddy be there too? I don't want to see Daddy, not like that. They were mean to him, Momma. I don't think I want to go?" My voice is cracking as I cry.

"Okay Audrey, but like I said, honey, I just don't want to go alone. Your Daddy won't be there he's in jail, and until I get this done, he will have to stay there. I don't want to think of your Daddy sitting in Jail." She looked like she was going to cry.

"Alright, Momma I will go. You're sure he won't be there?" I just can't face Daddy in that place.

"That's what they told me, Honey. Now, get your coat; we need to go." Momma sounds much happier.

My Aunt Reba came to stay with the little ones. Momma is telling her she can't go through this anymore. She said Daddy's brothers has to do something with him. It is hard enough working and taking care of six kids. She just isn't going to do this anymore. Aunt Reba hugs her and tells her she had better get going. Momma says she needs to drop the other kids off at school first, and she isn't sure how long she would be gone.

I heard Aunt Reba ask Momma, "Are sure Carly that Audrey should go with you? From what you said, Cameron is mad at the girls, too." Aunt Reba had one hand on her hip and a cigarette in the other.

"Yes, it will be all right, Reba. Cameron won't be there. Besides, I think it would help if the judge sees one of the kids at least." Ah, so that's why I'm going, but I'm sure she doesn't want to go alone either.

"Oh, you're probably right. Yeah, Audrey will be fine. I've always thought she was your most serious child. You look at her, and you never know what she's thinking. She always seems to be so guarded." I was watching Aunt Jean's cigarette. Every time she said something; she would move her hand that held the cigarette. I just knew she was going to burn herself.

Momma glanced over at me and said, "She takes after her Daddy there. All she does is read, and she finds some of the things her Dad talks about; while he's ranting, interesting." That was true. Not everything Daddy talked about was crazy. Some of it made sense.

Carmen stuck her head out the car window and told momma they were going to be late for school. Momma told Aunt Reba bye and hurried to get in the car. Of course, my Aunt had a few bad names to call my Daddy; before we left, but I want to repeat them. Aunt Reba is a beautiful woman on the outside with fiery red hair, but and a temper to go with it. We all knew that, even her kids. That's the kind of person she was. What you see, is what you get. No one messed with my Aunt Reba. We knew when Aunt Reba watched us we had better be good. Not that she ever hit us, but we knew she would. Oddly enough, I always know it's my Aunt Reba I can count on if I needed her, but at the same time, I'm afraid of her. Afraid of what she might have to do to protect us, if she could or would. No, I wasn't going to take that chance. I couldn't lose my brothers and sisters.

All we have is each other. Carmen, Ceely and I know we have to protect the little ones. I know we are barely capable of helping ourselves much less them, but we are all they have. I know that I would die fighting before I let one of them get hurt, or taken away.

The ride to downtown Dallas is very quiet. I enjoy riding through Dallas; the buildings seem majestic. There they stand, tall and proud. Through stormy and windy weather, they hold their ground. Some look brand new and shiny, even though they were very old. Others look their age, but still stood as proud as the day they were built. Daddy once told me that the downtown area of a city was its backbone. The buildings represent its strength. If that's true, Dallas was certainly a mighty city. My favorite building is the Texaco building. You can see the horse with wings on top, way before you see the building itself. Momma say's that it's a Unicorn, but it looked like a red horse to me. I thought it was a pretty neat building.

As Momma leaves the freeway; she points out for me, where President Kennedy's car will be coming through Dallas. He will be in Dallas next week. Everybody is talking about it. My teacher said we should feel honored, and I do. We knew who our president is. Daddy and Momma made sure we watched all his speeches, on TV. I thought he was a very nice man that wanted everybody to get along, and care for each other. I knew he was a man to be respected and looked up to like my Granddaddy. Momma liked him, but not as much as Daddy did. She said there was some thing's he said she didn't agree with, but overall she liked him. I think everybody did.

When I got out of the car, I looked over to where the Presidents parade would be. There is a lot of people everywhere you look. How exciting it would be to be able to be here. I'm suddenly jerked out of my day dreaming by Momma.

"C'mon Audrey, you're going to get lost, and we are late." She was pulling me by my arm toward an old building that looked like a castle.

At the top of the stairs, momma stopped for a minute and looked around. She took a deep breath and we walked inside. Once inside I'm immediately scared. I knew I was in an adult world. It seems like we have to go up a thousand stairs before we get to the room Momma has to see the Judge. There are policemen in the hallway. They have guns in their holsters, just like the cowboy movies. Everything seemed big here. The courtroom was dark and seems shadowy. At one end there is this big desk that almost covers the man sitting behind it. Next to his desk is a chair. There are two tables that sit across from the big desk with chairs behind them. People are sitting at them. Behind the tables, at the back of the room, there are rows of long benches. They are set up, so the big desk divides them. You can walk between them and sit to your left or right. A man came up and asked Momma her name. When she told him, he told us to sit on the front bench on the right. Momma asked if it mattered where?

"He said no just take a seat." Of course, Momma has to sit us at the beginning of the row.

There is a low wall with a swinging door that separates us from the people who sit at the tables. People came in and sat all around us. Soon all the benches were full. I looked over at Momma. She was looking straight ahead, somewhere above where the man sat behind the big desk. Momma looks worried. I feel really small in this room. Maybe Momma does, too. I reached over and took her hand. She gives my hand a gentle squeeze and places her hands together, in her lap. I know Momma is afraid, and I don't blame her. It's okay to be afraid. I am, and I don't have to get up and talk to anyone. I looked around the room to avoid looking at Momma. It is dark in here. The only light is coming through the two big windows on the right side of the room. I stare at the shadows of the light for a while. It is coming through in four long stripes. Between each stripe, there is a dark shadow. Inside the stripes, there are little shiny particles floating around. I wonder if I walk over and take a deep breath will the tiny particles go inside me? I want to go and run my hand through them to see if my hand will disappear. A man calling out Mommas name brought my attention back to where I am. I see Momma stand to walk to where the judge sits, behind the big desk. When she reached the spot with the swinging door, Momma stops and looks to her left. Following her gaze, I caught my breath. Daddy was sitting there between two men. Momma hesitated a second then walked on.

The man said for her to sit in the chair by the judge. I sat frozen looking at the back of the chair my Daddy is sitting in. Daddy turns and smiles at me, but he looks sad. Forcing myself to turn away I look at

Momma. She is talking to the judge. She told him about Daddy locking us up for three weeks. She's telling him about the time Daddy locked us in for three weeks. She says there were times when he wouldn't let us eat and that he used bad language with his girls and talked crazy. At this point, she nods toward me. The judge looked over and then tells momma to go on. She says he blames her and their daughters for all his problems. Momma says he would beat her in front of us kids. She tells him she is afraid of my daddy and what he might do to her. That struck me as strange. I never saw my Momma as being afraid of my Daddy. She always stood up to him, even when he hit her, she fought back. The only time I remember her being afraid is when he first locked us all in the house; even then, she tried to fight back, this isn't the Momma I know. She's crying and twisting a handkerchief in her lap, pleading with the judge. My Momma is one of those people who can cry and still look beautiful. She's convincing, too. I'm confused, is this my Mother? Is Momma afraid of Daddy as we are? Maybe she didn't want us to see how frightened of Daddy she was. Maybe for us, she had to pretend to be strong so that we wouldn't be scared. *Oh Momma, are you just acting?* I know how important it is for the judge to believe her. That's the most important thing, for the judge to understand how dangerous my Daddy can be. A man sitting at the table in front of us told Momma she could step down.

The man called Daddy to come up front. Daddy's hands are in chains, and his clothes look different. There is a tag on the front of his shirt with some numbers on it. I feel sorry for him.

I want to jump up and say, "Let him go!" Instead, I say to Momma, "Can we go now? Please, Momma, I want to leave this place."

She shook her head and whispered, "I do too, but we can't.

Daddy sat in the big chair by the judge. He's telling him he can't cope with losing his father in February. He wants to protect his family. Daddy tells them he thinks some people are going to take us away like they did his father. He says he can't live without his family. If he lets us go outside something bad will happen to us. Daddy says he is sorry, and he won't act like that again.

Daddy is told to step down. The judge tells a man sitting next to Daddy that

Cameron Olsen is to be sent to Terrell State Hospital for evaluation. He says Daddy shows signs of a nervous breakdown due to the death of his father. According to an evaluation from Parkland Hospital he also shows signs of depression and despondency. I asked Momma what that meant? She told me to be quiet. She would tell me later. The Judge says as he hits a little hammer on the desk, that court would take a break and resume after lunch. The man sitting with Daddy walked over and whispered something to Momma.

"Audrey, Daddy wants to tell us goodbye. Do you want to talk to him?" She seems nervous.

"Okay, Momma. We can do that, but I don't want him to touch me." At that moment I wasn't scared of Daddy. I think he was scared of me.

Momma walks up to Daddy. He's asking her why is she doing this to him? She said he needs help. She told him we have to go now. Daddy took a step toward me. He then bent down to kiss me.

Turning away I say, "Bye Daddy, I hope they can make you well." I don't know what else to say. It hurt treating Daddy this way, but I feel if I let Daddy kiss me he would think everything he had done was okay, and it wasn't!

Once in the car, I turn to Momma, "I thought you said Daddy wouldn't be there? What happened?" I was trembling.

"I know honey; that threw me for a loop, too. My Lawyer told me Daddy wouldn't be there, I promise. I'm sorry you had to see him, but everything went okay didn't it?" Momma was back to being strong again; this was the Momma I knew.

"I guess so, but Momma I will never forget the look on Daddy's face. It was so sad and confused. Like he didn't understand why he was there." I said this in almost a whisper. My heart was breaking for my Daddy.

When we got home, I had to relive the day all over again; while Momma told Aunt Reba how it went. Carmen was sitting on the couch holding Craig. Ceely had just walked in from the bedroom where she had changed out of her school dress. Ceely hated wearing dresses. Momma called her a *tomboy*. The rest of the kids were playing outside. I was relieved when she asked Ceely and me to walk to the store and get her some Dr. Pepper and cigarettes. While we were walking, at first we didn't talk. Ceely kept kicking this rock in front of her.

Finally, I said. "Ceely is it bad for me to be happy that Daddy won't be home for a while? I mean, today when Momma and I walked in the house, everything seemed so normal. It felt right. The house seemed happy." I had to break the silence. I thought, maybe she is mad at me, for going.

Ceely stopped kicking her rock and said quietly, "I don't know, but I feel the same way. You know, we'll have to move again. We always do." Then she said she was going to her friends' house. Ceely said to tell Momma for her, and took off running.

I watched her until she disappeared over the low wooden fence that separated the churchyard from the sidewalk. She jumps over that fence without even touching it. There isn't a boy around that can beat my sister at anything. She runs faster. Jumps higher and can whip any of them if they make her mad enough, or if they pick on anyone in our family. Ceely has had more scrapes, bruises, and broken bones than any of us, but she's tough. No one goes up against a dare with Ceely, because they know she will do it and beat them at it. Having Ceely as a big sister is better than any big brother I could have had. It's not that she looks like a boy either. She has to try real hard to be *boyish*. That's another thing you don't say to Ceely. Never tell her how pretty she is, or else she will come after you.

Chapter 8

"She thinks the pain is over., She's naive.
She believes in a dream world; only she can see.
They will shatter her dreams, for they are not naïve."

Today is November the 22nd. Daddy is at Terrell State Hospital. Momma says they are helping him. I wonder what kind of medicine you can take for your brain. *Ceely is right* we are going to move this weekend, but it's not far. We will still be in the same school district, so happy I won't have to tell my friends. They will never know I moved. No one knows where I live, to begin with, since I can never invite anyone over.

This morning I made a new friend on the playground. She's a lot bigger and older than me, but she is in the fifth grade too. People say she is, *retarded.* I think she just thinks slower than we do. Some kids make fun of her. This morning she is standing in the middle of the playground with her head tilted to one side on her shoulder, slowly turning around in circles singing and talking to herself. Some boy's thought it would be funny to circle her and call her names. They scared her, so she starts yelling. I told them to leave her alone and grabbed her hand to pull her away. She hit at me, but that was okay I knew she was afraid.

As we are walking off one of the boy's screams at me, "You're *retarded*, too."

Then another one says, "No, you're not retarded, you're *just white trash.*

Then the first boy says, "What's the difference." I didn't let them see that their words bothered me.

They were just trying to hurt my feelings. I wasn't about to show them that they had.

My new friend keeps saying, "Mean boys," over and over."

What was sad about it too, one of those mean boys is her brother. When I finally get her to calm down, the bell rings to go inside. I told her my name and asked her what hers was. She told me her Mommy calls her Chloe Ann, but I am supposed to call her just, Chloe. I smiled at her as her teacher walks up to take Chloe to class. I say I would see her at lunch.

Chloe hugs her teacher and says, "I have a new friend her name is Audrey. My Mommy calls me Chloe Ann, but my new friend has to call me Chloe. I don't like boys.

They're always mean to me. I don't like my brother sometimes either." She keeps talking as they walk off.

Chloe is telling her the mean boys said her new friend was white trash, but she didn't think her new friend heard them. She said she knew this was a bad name because they sometimes call her that too. Her teacher turns to look out at the playground to see if she could find these boys and then she turns to me and gives me a sad smile as we enter the building.

Something my Daddy had once told me entered my head. I don't remember exactly when, but he said there's always someone who is going to have a harder road to cross than you.

"Well, I guess I just met that someone, Daddy." I hadn't realized I had said it out loud until Robbie walks up to me. He was a friend of mine from music class.

"Hey Audrey, you talking to yourself again?" He was grinning at me.

"Yeah, I guess I am. I was thinking about something my Daddy had once said to me." I smiled at him. Robbie could always make me laugh.

"Boy, you're different from me. I try not to think about the things my Dad says to me.

It's after I have made him mad, and it sure wouldn't make me smile or him either." We laugh and walk into our music class.

We had just sat down when the Principal came over the loud speaker. It soundds like he is crying. His voice keeps making that cracking sound. He said that they were closing school early today.

"There has been a tragedy in downtown Dallas. The President of the United States has been shot. President John F. Kennedy has died at Parkland Hospital. Please listen to your teachers and leave the school in an orderly fashion. If anyone needs their parents called to pick them up, please come by the school's office. What a sad day for Dallas and America. This day November 22nd, 1963 will go down in our history books. We will let your parents know when school will resume." All you heard after that was the secretary crying and then the speaker clicked off.

Everyone in the classroom just sat there for a moment. No one moved. It seems like we were all afraid to take a breath. Then the teacher cleared her throat and told us to bow our heads in prayer. Her voice sounded so sweet and sad, asking God to protect the Presidents' wife and young children. She also asked God to forgive the person who did this to him and to see all the children home safely to their parents. I started to cry. Most of the class was crying by then, even some of the tough boys.

Mrs. Fields raises her head and says through her tears," I want you all to gather your books and take them to your lockers. Do not take any home with you. Now, line up by the door, and class I'm so sorry you had to lose such a wonderful President. He was trying to make a brighter future for you. Always remember him this way." She hugged each one of us as we walked out the door.

A little girl in front of me, her name was Sandra, stopped to hug Mrs. Fields. She told her, "Don't cry; God has a plan for all of us. It will be okay."

Mrs. Fields hugged her back, "Thank you, honey. I know he does." For the first time since the announcement our teacher smiled.

Once outside I didn't know what to do. Robbie stood with me for a while, until his mother came. I knew my Momma wasn't coming. She was working. I couldn't find Ceely, so I walk home. It is quiet; there aren't very many cars out like there usually is. I guess everybody is home watching their TV. When I got home, the whole family is there, even Momma. She is sitting on the couch crying, so are Carmen and Ceely. The man on TV said this day would go down in history, as *the day America cried*. I was scared. I didn't know what to think. It was one thing for me to have to deal with something bad happening to me, but when everyone in America was crying, I didn't know what to do. Adults don't cry like this. They're supposed to be strong. Even the announcers on the television are crying. I didn't know what to think. There isn't a station on TV that didn't have something about President Kennedy on it. Only now they are calling him the *late President Kennedy*. They said, the man who shot him had been killed. People seemed happy about it. That scared me too. There was only one thing I knew for sure; as the newsman said, America would never be the same again.

The next weekend Momma let Cossette, and I go to Grandmothers' for a visit. The Presidents funeral is on TV. His little girl and boy were holding their Mommas' hand. They look scared and sad. The little boy is called, *John John*. A man handed him a United States Flag.

"Grandmother those kids are so brave, I don't know if I could do that." I start to cry. I feel sorry for President Kennedy's family.

"Granddaddy, why do nice people have to die?" I sat down cross-legged in front of the TV. I'm thinking of all the nice things the President had tried to do for all the people in our country.

"I don't know Audrey. Why don't you and Cossette go outside and play? Little children shouldn't be watching this." My first thought was to tell him I wasn't a child.

I was ten years old, but then we were always taught not to talk back to our elders, especially Granddaddy. I rolled my eyes at Cossette and told her to come on. About the same time, the doorbell rang, and it was my friends.

Grandmother and Grand-daddy stayed in front of the television the rest of the day. Grandmother only got up to cook. Cossette and I played in the backyard with my friends, Jasmin and Franny; for a while, we didn't have to think about what had happened. We just played. Cossette is hard to play with she always wants things her way. If she didn't get it, she would start calling me names and make fun of my scars where I had been burned. My friends usually ended up going home. I don't know why Cossette was like that, but I knew she was just a little kid. It hurt though because she was my sister. We went home on Sunday. On Monday we got to go back to school.

After three months Daddy got out of the hospital, and yes Momma lets him come home. He seemed okay. Daddy was okay for a long time after that. He tried to help me understand the death of our President and why sometimes there just isn't a reason when bad things happen to good people. Sometimes Daddy would say some crazy things that didn't make sense to me, but I knew someday they would. He told me the Doctors said he was Paranoid Schizophrenic, and that he would be on medication the rest of his life. If he didn't take it, he would get bad again. I told him I would help him *remember* because I didn't want ever to see the mean Daddy again. Our family seemed normal or as normal as we usually were. Momma and Daddy still fought, usually over him losing another job. Momma would throw Daddy out of the house for a few days. He would stay with one of his brothers, but he didn't have to go back to the hospital. Momma always would let him come back. To me this year was full of changes. We lost a President in a way I never would have thought could happen, and my Parents no longer loved each other. It was as if Momma didn't care about Daddy anymore. I think she wanted him to leave for good.

I like being in the sixth grade. I get to be in more activities at school. Plus, the teachers treat me differently. I'm in the highest grade of the school, so you get to have more responsibilities. The only bad part is, I have to miss more school to stay home and babysit when one of the younger kids are sick. It's hard to feel part of a class when you're not able to be there all the time. I also fall behind. It's embarrassing to come back to school after missing three or four days, and you don't know what page the class is on. It never fails; the teacher always picks on me to read. I have always been good in Literature and English. Those were my most favorite subjects, and it seems to learn them came naturally to me. By sixth grade, I know now what I want to be when I grow up, a Writer. I know I'm better at expressing my feelings on paper than vocally. I love reading poetry and short stories. Finally, I got smart and started taking all my books home with me. I never know when Momma is going to make me stay home, with one of the little ones. I also got a couple of phone numbers from the *bookworms* in my class; they're the ones who are smart. Of course, it isn't like attending class every day; there was still a lot I missed. I love learning, though. Even at my age, I know education is the way out for me. Daddy taught me that. Like I said, some of the things he talks about made since. I knew at an early age, to be able to have control of me, I had to understand other people, and why they do the things they do. Daddy taught me never to blame my problems on someone else. If I make a mistake, just admit it and go on. He said no one was to blame for the things he did; which I thought was strange because when he is sick, he blames us all. Daddy said, never to think that someone is better than me because of the clothes they wear, or where they live. It only means they have money. It's what's on the inside that counts. Yes, I learned a lot from my Daddy that year more than he could or would ever know.

January of 1964 is bitterly cold. People say it is the coldest winter we have had in years. Of course, I have to walk home from school. My coat is a hand me down, so it doesn't keep me very warm. The wind felt like it is going right through my skin to my bones. When I get home, the door is locked, so I bang on it to get Daddy's attention. He was out of work again. I can hear the TV going, but no one answered the door, so I walk around back. As I opened the screen door to the porch, I see newspaper all over the floor. *What a mess*, I thought. *I know what I will be doing as soon as I change.* The back porch door led right into the bedroom my sisters, and I share, so I throw my books down and go looking for someone to yell at for not letting me in. When I get to the living room Junior, Cossette and Craig are watching a cartoon on television.

"Didn't Y'all hear me banging on the door? It's cold out there, and I had to walk all the way from school. Where is everybody? Where is Daddy?" I gave them my sternest expression with my hands on my hips.

"Uh, Daddy told us not to answer the door. He said it was somebody who was probably coming to take him away again. He wouldn't even let me look out the window. Audrey, Daddy, kept us out of school today." Junior seems nervous, and he kept looking at Momma and Daddy's bedroom door.

"Oh. I'm sorry I got upset then. Does Momma know? Where is a Daddy?" I'm trying not to sound worried.

Junior pointed toward their bedroom. I turn and walk in that direction; as I got closer, I could smell the strong odor of cigarette smoke. The door is closed, so I knock. It always made Momma mad when Daddy would stay in the bedroom for hours. When Daddy got sick, he would start putting his cigarettes out on the floor, and he can be so messy.

Carmen, Ceely and I can tell when Daddy isn't taking his medicine. I got really good at reading Daddy's different moods. He had at least three. It was as if he had three different people inside of him. One-day Daddy would be sweet and helpless as a child. He would act afraid of everyone and everything. The next he could be overbearing and religious. Everything, he said or did is with his bible in hand. The third daddy is just evil. That's all I can say about him. We all knew to hide when Daddy was in this mood.

I knocked lightly on his bedroom door again. I didn't know which Daddy was in there, so I was trying not to upset him.

"Daddy it's Audrey. Are you okay? Can I come in?" I stood there for a while. When he didn't answer, I went to my bedroom to change clothes.

I told the kids that I was going to clean the back porch before Momma gets home. Carmen and Ceely should be home soon, and they will start dinner. I heard Craig and Junior play fighting. Okay, everything was normal again. I start picking up the paper; then Daddy storms through the back door to the porch.

"What do you think you're doing, Audrey Rose? Don't touch these newspapers. They need to stay there, covering the floor, for our protection. I know you're not old enough to know how our Government works, but they can spy on us. I put the papers out here so their radar can't find us. You know they want to take my family away from me, and I won't let them. They'll have to kill me first." I stop picking up newspapers and start shaking at the word, *kill*.

There's a sense of anger in every word that was coming out of Daddy's mouth, but the word *kill* is spat out between clenched teeth. Daddy believes every word he says, and I know he will do exactly, what he says.

"Okay Daddy, it'll be okay. I'll just put these back where you had them." I slowly let the papers drop from my hands.

I know for certain now that my Daddy isn't taking his medication, again. It happened before, but this time seems worse. I take his hand and lead him back into the house. I hope he isn't feeling how bad I'm shaking. He walks right back to his bedroom and shuts the door, but not before telling me he is hungry.

He gave me a look of confusion and says, "Audrey, when did you get home? Do you know when your Mother will be here? I need to let her know why the kids didn't go to school today. Junior kept them out, and this is nonsense. She needs to get better control of him but tell her she doesn't have to punish him. I took my belt to him. The Bible says, spare the rod spoil the child. I made sure he won't skip school again. Call me when dinner is ready."

Just that fast Daddy changed as if the conversation on the back porch never happened. I spun around and hurried to the living room. The kids are still watching TV.

"Junior come here a minute. I need to talk to you. Come in the kitchen." He looks at me and rolls his eyes, but he gets up off the couch and follows me into the kitchen. I thought I saw a wince as he got up.

"Junior Daddy said he spanked you with his belt today for skipping school. Did he?" I said this with disbelief in my voice.

Daddy has never hit us. He might have done other things, but he never hit us. Well, not me I guess.

"So, what if he did hit me; wouldn't be the first time; besides I didn't want him to hurt Craig or Cossette. He didn't hurt me. Just scared them."

"I'm sorry, I didn't know. Raise your shirt so I can see how bad it is. You may need to see a doctor." I reached for his shirt, but he pushed my hand away.

"I said it was no big deal. I'm just fine. When's dinner." With that said he flopped back down on the couch. Giving Craig a shove to get out of his way.

When Momma got home, I told her how Daddy was acting. She said she was afraid that he hadn't been taking his medicine, and that they would talk tonight about him going back to the hospital. By that night there was no talking to the *man* that calls himself our Daddy. The last thing I remember before falling to sleep was Daddy yelling at Momma. He said she just wanted to get rid of him so her boyfriend can move in. He said he knew she didn't love him anymore and that she was seeing someone else. My last thought before drifting off was, *same old same old.* They will never change.

The next thing I know I smell smoke and my throat is burning. Momma is shaking us awake and telling us to run and get out of the house it was on fire. By the time we got outside the fire trucks had pulled up. After they had put it out the fire, they said we could go back inside; that it had been contained to the back porch. I look around for Daddy. He was sitting in the back of a police car. Our eyes met, and he knows I know what he has done. He never took his eyes off my face. Finally, I look away. I put my arms around Cossette, and we slowly walk back into the house.

Once inside I ask Momma, "How many more times are we going to have to go through this? Next time, he just might kill us."

Momma says she wants Carmen, Ceely and me to put the kids back to bed, and then come back; she needs to talk to us.

"You girls won't have to go through this with your Dad again. I am going to divorce him this time. He will never get to live with us again." Just like that, Momma had made up her mind.

The relief we were feeling is almost audible. I just wanted normal in my life. I didn't want to be afraid to go to sleep ever again. The house was filled with the smell of burnt paper and wood, but we stayed there. We had nowhere else to go. Daddy went back to Terrell State Hospital, and we moved, again. I didn't care at this point If I ever saw my Daddy again. I told Momma this, and she said I shouldn't feel that way. My Daddy is sick, and he can't help the things he does, but I knew different. Didn't he say no one was to blame for his problems but himself? All I know is that daddy tried to burn me to death. I guess he thought being burned at three wasn't bad enough. It will take me a long time to get over this, but I knew I would; *after all our Daddy is sick, and somehow we are to blame for it.*

Chapter 9

"How far will you go, when you can't turn back? How high will you jump, just because they tell you, too? How can your life turn upside down when it's never been right?"

Momma hasn't gotten a divorce from Daddy yet, but she won't let him come home either. Daddy was right; Momma has a boyfriend. I haven't met him yet, but I know she has one. She bought a car from him; that's how she met him. A used *car salesman*, that's what Ceely says he is. Momma brought his little dog to our house, too. Get this; Ceely says he's married, and his wife doesn't like the dog. When Momma finally got around to telling us about him, she said he was getting a divorce, just like her and Daddy. I don't know what to think. The memory of Daddy being out of our house hasn't even sunk in yet; now she wants to bring a total stranger into our life. She says we will like him. He loves kids.

When I first meet him, I feel uneasy. I'm not sure why, but there is something about him that makes me feel nervous. He scares me for some reason, and Ceely too.

When Momma introduces him to me, he says, "*Audie*, nice to meet you." I shiver.

I don't know why it's just the way he looks at me, and the way his voice changes when he says my nickname. *Only those I love can call me that, not him!* Well, it just made my skin crawl. He will also grab at Momma in front of us kids. It seems he always looks around first to make sure we are watching. Momma says his name is, *Freddy*.

Carmen is dating this nice guy named Robin, at the time Momma started seeing Freddy. Carmen doesn't even look up while Momma is introducing Freddy, or she's pretended not to care. Ceely is dating, too. She is dating a guy named, Levi. We feel like he's part of the family. Robin is too. Us kids adore Robin and Levi. They're the only friends Momma let come over, ever so often, but they're here enough to feel like part of the family.

Things are changing drastically at home. Sadly, now that Momma sees more of Freddy, she doesn't let Levi and Robin come over as often. We still get to visit Daddy. Momma takes us out to Terrell

Hospital to have picnics with him. We even spent Easter Sunday with him, but we were told by Momma never to mention Freddy's name to Daddy. Daddy seems happy here. He always tells us how much he loves us, and he begs Momma to let him come home. I know Daddy will never be welcome at our house, again. I hate visiting Daddy in this place. Heck, I hate anybody having to be here. I feel sad, and it scares me at the same time. If you have never been to a State Hospital for the mentally insane; it will be hard for you to understand how I feel.

I get chills as we drive down the small lanes past all the buildings with bars on their windows. We have to drive all the way to the back of the property to get to where Daddy is kept. One building which is three stories high houses the criminally insane, that's what Daddy says anyway. This building scares me the most. It looks very old and spooky. There's ugly green stuff that grows on the outside walls. Carmen says it's called Moss. All I know is it smells funny and is scary. The people inside look out at us as we drive past. I wonder what it looks like at night here, and I shudder.

The area Daddy stays in looks newer, but once inside I can tell, they don't take care of it. The walls are all painted the same, drab tan. If they are trying to make, people feel better. The walls would be painted a brighter color. Daddy never wants us to walk him back to the ward because he said they put crazy people in there with him. That makes me laugh. He won't let any of the patients talk to us either; except this one lady. He always seems proud when he introduces us to her. Of course, he says there is nothing wrong with her either. Her family put her here for the same reason Momma put him here. They don't want her around anymore. In a way, I believe him, because after Daddy has been here for a few days, it seems like nothing is wrong with him. Maybe, there *is* something wrong with our family that makes Daddy crazy. He never acts as bad when he stays with his brothers or mother, just when he would come home to us.

In a couple of months, I will be twelve. Daddy got out of the hospital this week. He is staying with his Mother. Someone in his family must have told him about Freddy, because when Daddy came over today, he is mad. He and Momma are in an argument on our front lawn. She is telling him she deserves to have a life with whom she pleases and that he cannot come over anymore. She says, she is going to get something from the Courts to prevent him from coming and that they would arrest him if he comes back.

Daddy is furious when he says to her, "You can't keep me from seeing the kids, Carly!" He took a step toward Momma.

She yells for Carmen to call the police. "Cameron! I not only can keep you from your kids, but I will if you don't leave this minute. If you keep this up, I will demand child support too." Carmen was standing on the porch as if rooted in place.

"Okay, I'm leaving. Carly, don't keep the kids from me." Daddy knew Momma would do what she said. He also knew she could, too.

True to her word, Momma has filed for divorce against Daddy. Momma let us see Daddy, whenever it was convenient for her, which is quite a bit.

By this time Freddy has been in our lives for a year. I'm twelve now, and guess who lives with us? I just thought it was a nightmare living with Daddy. Now, there is a stranger living in our house. A stranger that just loves little kids, *actually teenage girls*. Freddy, also wants us to call him,

Sugar Daddy, Yuk! I don't like to complain; especially to Momma, but I can't do this. I learned at a very early age that if I stayed quiet and did what I'm told no one will bother me, but I just can't bring myself to call him that.

I tell Momma how I feel, "Momma I don't want to call Freddy, 'Sugar Daddy.' That's weird don't you think?"

Cossette and I are sitting at the table peeling potatoes. Cossette pipes up and says, "Well, I'm sure not going to call him that. He's not *sweet* like *sugar* and Freddy sure ain't my *Daddy!*" I love how outspoken Cossette can be.

Whatever's on her mind will just come flying out of her mouth. I thought Momma was going to smack her. Cossette is seven years old now and full of, *spit and vinegar*, as our Granddaddy likes to say.

"You just watch your mouth Cossette and don't you ever talk like that to Freddy, again. If nothing else, I taught you kids to show respect to adults. Do you hear me? Wipe that smirk off your face before I do it for you." Oh man, Momma is mad now. She turns to me, and if looks can kill, I would be dead.

I frown at Cossette and brace for Mommas wrath. "Audrey Rose, it isn't going to hurt you to call Freddy *sugar daddy* if that's what he wants. Don't you kids want me to be happy? No! Y'all would prefer if I were miserable just like your Daddy does. Well, I'm not living that way anymore, and your Daddy is not coming back!" With that, she pushes her chair back and walks off. The next thing we hear is her bedroom door slam.

"Wow, look what you started and they say you're the quiet one. You're supposed to be the good daughter. I'm still not going to call Freddy *sugar daddy*. How about you, Audie?" Okay, so I do not like my little sister's outspokenness right about now.

"Me! You're the one that got her upset. Thanks a lot, and no I'm not calling him that. He's too weird for me. None of us will call him that. I don't know what Momma is thinking. He's nothing like Daddy. I mean when Daddy is well." I just want to scream.

What was Momma thinking? I didn't want my Daddy and her to live together again, ever. Things are much better with them apart. They get along better, and it is nicer to visit Daddy than have him live with us. No, I don't want Daddy to come home. The little one's blame Momma for Daddy being put in the hospital. They don't remember how bad he could be, and that's okay. They think they have the best Daddy in the world, and I will never tell them any different. I'm deep in thought when I hear Cossette talking again.

"Audie, I do miss Daddy. I wish he could live with Momma and us. I wish Momma would make that man leave." Sometimes Cossette just broke my heart. I would forget how hurtful she can be.

"I know Cossette, but he can't, and I don't think Momma will make Freddy leave. Maybe, just maybe, he will get tired of all us kids. C'mon, let's get the potatoes on before Momma comes back." We had just stood when Freddy walks into the front door.

"Who's gonna make who leave?" Freddy follows us into the kitchen. I tell Cossette I will finish; she can play. She didn't hesitate.

"Oh, no one. We were just talking. Momma's in her bedroom." I get so nervous when Freddy is in the room.

Freddy steps behind me. I'm at the sink rinsing the potatoes. He put his hand on my shoulder and leans over the sink to face me. I drop the pan and back away. Something about the way he touched me made me shake.

"What's wrong Audie? Are you afraid of me? You don't have to be you know. I'm not gonna hurt you. I promise I won't bite; only if you want me too." He had a strange look on his face, and his voice dropped on the last part of his sentence.

I have never been talked to like that before. I don't know how to take what Freddy said, but I know it doesn't sound right.

"No. No, Freddy, I'm not afraid of you. I just didn't hear you come up behind me. I've got to finish dinner." Oh good I thought, he's leaving.

At the kitchen door, he turns and says. "Oh, and by the way I'm not going anywhere. I like living here with your mother and her girls." Then he was gone.

I just want to cry. What has Momma done? I'm going to talk to Carmen and Ceely. They'll know what to do. I find Ceely first, and tell her what happened; she says I should tell Momma. I know that won't do any good, though. Not after how mad she got when I told her I didn't want to call Freddy, *sugar daddy*. I know she will think I'm making it up because I don't want her to be happy, as she put it. So I will say nothing, besides Momma works hard, I don't want to upset her anymore. She's right she deserves to be happy; after what Daddy has put her through. I know she's done everything she can to keep us together as a family. I guess I should be thankful for that. Maybe I'm just overreacting, but I still refuse to call Freddy anything, but *Freddy*.

Chapter 10

"She was supposed to protect them.
She was the only one that could.
Then why were they left alone, facing the wolf?"

We are having a carnival at school; I'm excited. During P.E. we were taught to square dance. The best groups get to dance for the parents coming to the carnival, and my group will be one of them. I enjoy dancing oh any kind. We learned to Waltz and Polka too, but square dancing is my favorite. I love the outfits we get to wear; white blouses with puffy sleeves, and a red paisley skirt. The bandanas we wear in our hair are made from the same design and material as our skirt. Our socks are white with red lace and white tennis shoes. The boys are wearing white shirts with black pants. One of the mothers made our skirts for us. The only bad thing was that we had to pay for our outfits. We couldn't afford it, so my teacher was nice enough to pay for mine. Momma said I couldn't be in it at first. Momma said we didn't have the money for something I would only wear once. I was so upset I cried when I told the teacher. She sent a note home to Momma saying she needed me to be in it and if it were okay with her she would buy the material for my skirt and everything else I would need. At first, Momma didn't want her to, but after a lot of crying and begging on my part, she said okay.

On the night of the carnival, everything that could go wrong did. The boy I was supposed to have as my partner; who by the way was the cutest boy in school, got sick and couldn't come, so I had to dance with the alternant boy. When we had practiced, our alternates had to stand in sometimes. All of us girls were so hoping none of our partners would get sick that night because the alternant was Richard, my friend Chloe's brother. He knew we didn't want to dance with him, and why. He was obnoxious; didn't take practice seriously, and tried jokingly to make a girl he was dancing with trip and fall over his feet. When I got to the school gym that night, Richard was standing there with a big grin on his face. I wanted to cry. I had already told everybody that I was going to get my hair fixed real pretty for the dance. Carmen was going to curl it for me, but she didn't get home on time, so I had to throw my hair up in a ponytail as usual. Then Momma called and said she wasn't going to get to come because she had to work late. I pulled part of the hem out of my skirt while I was getting dressed, and Ceely had to fix it for me. I was in tears by the time I got to the school that night. My brothers and sisters were the only ones that got to come and watch me dance. That's how our life always was, just us kids. When I walk into the gym; where we were to dance, I was told about Richard. I break down and cry.

The girls gather around me, and were all speaking at once, "Audrey, it will be all right. Maybe Richard will be serious tonight; after all, surely he won't embarrass himself by messing around while dancing."

"Y'all can say that because y'all don't have to dance with him! I do! I'm going home!" There are tears streaming down my face, as I turn to run, but was stopped by my teacher.

"Audrey, calm down, honey. Don't let something like this stand in your way. Everything will be fine, I promise. Honey, never give up on something you've worked hard to achieve. Audrey, you're not a quitter. Now dry your eyes and let's show them how good we are." She's right I did work hard on this routine.

It wasn't easy remembering all those dance steps, and I can't let the others down in my group. Hurrying to step into formation alongside Richard I felt nervous, but he gave me a big smile and motions for me to hurry. Maybe it will be all right, after all. It isn't just all right; it is great. Richard dances very well. He didn't forget any of the steps, and he didn't make me trip and fall. Everybody clapped for us and said we did wonderfully. Afterward, Richard thanked me for dancing with him and said, he was proud to have been my partner. I know I must have looked like an idiot because I just stood there and stared at him; this can't be the same obnoxious boy that picks on me all the time. I finally said he was welcome, and that I was glad he got to be my partner. I was. All of us had a lot of fun that night. We got free tickets because I had participated in the event. The neatest part was when I won a great big chocolate cake, playing the cakewalk game. Number 19 was the number they called when the music stopped, and I was standing on it. I decided right then that 19 would always be my lucky number. I went to bed that night feeling special for the first time in my life. By Monday morning Richard was back to his obnoxious self, but I knew that it was just an act he had to put on in front of the other boy's. Nothing he did bothered me anymore. I knew we were friends in a strange way.

Things at home were changing. Carmen isn't dating Robin, anymore. I remember hearing her, Momma and Freddy arguing one night. Brenda told Momma she wasn't fair.

"Momma, I love him, and he loves me." Carmen sounds like she is going to cry.

Momma replied tiredly, "Carmen you're only fourteen. You're too young to know what love is."

I know Carmen loves Robin, we all did. Carmen cried a lot after that night. Momma made her break up with Robin.

Carmen went to live with Daddy after that. He was staying with my Maw Maw and my Uncle Herman. My uncle was the fourth in line of my Maw Maw's sons. He was the only one of her son's that never married. He almost did once, but his fiancé left him standing at the Alter. That's what everyone told me. I realized there was something wrong with him. I'm not sure what it was, but he always acted younger than what he was. I don't mean young like a kid, but more like he was a kid. My older sisters and some of my girl cousins didn't like being around him alone. I had that same feeling, not that he had ever done anything to me, it was just a feeling I had. Carmen went to stay with them. She was hurt by what Momma made her do. I didn't want her to go. I understood why she went, but I didn't want her to go. I'm not too worried about being left there alone with Freddy. As long as Ceely, and I was there the little ones would be all right. By then we were aware that Freddy's interest was teenage girls.

Things were okay for a while; we moved into a nicer house. It was in Pleasant Grove, a suburb of Dallas, and I was starting seventh grade. While living here, I learned the ugly side of becoming a woman. One day all through school I had these cramps. I was worried. I thought I was getting sick, or that something was really bad wrong with me. As soon as I got home, I ran to the bathroom. I felt like I wet myself. When I look down at my pants, there is blood all over them. *Oh, my God, this is it I'm dying,* I thought. I didn't know what to do. I sat there until I hear Ceely come in, and I scream for her. When she comes to the bathroom door, it is locked. I'm afraid someone will walk in on me. I truly did not know what was wrong with me.

"Audie, what's wrong? Open the door. I hear you crying. I can't help you if you don't let me in. Do you want me to get Momma? Audrey! Let me in!" Ceely is getting very upset with me, by this time. I told her, no don't get Momma.

I unlock the door. Ceely, comes in and locks it back behind her, "Audie, did Freddy do something to you?" She looks ready to kill someone.

"NO! Oh no Ceely, but look. I think I'm dying. There's something wrong with me." I was scared.

I realized I had been sitting on the pot with my pants still on and my legs crossed. I slowly uncross my legs so Ceely could see how much blood there was.

"Oh, is that all. Audie, you're not dying. It's just, well you've gotten your monthly period. Didn't Mom tell you about this? You're a woman now." She was laughing, but when she saw the tears on my face, she stops.

"Here let me get you some pads. When a girl reaches a certain age, she starts her period. I did when I was 10, but that was young. All it means is now you can have babies." Ceely's voice and head lower as she says this. Then continues, "I was wondering when you were going to get yours. Here let me show you how to use these," Ceely hands me a long white pad, "and then I will go get you some clean clothes. You'll have to wash these right away in cold water or the stain won't come out." She left then, and I locked the door behind her.

Oh, great now I'm a woman, something to worry me. Okay now I can have babies, and I wonder just how is that supposed to happen. I started thinking how strange it was that so much goes on around me, and I don't even notice, or maybe I just don't question it. Why didn't Momma tell me about this or why didn't I notice when it happened to Carmen and Ceely? I had seen the pads before but never ask what they were. It doesn't surprise me though that Momma never talked to me about it. She doesn't talk to me about much of anything personal.

When Ceely came back, I asked her, "Ceely, how does a woman get pregnant?"

She looks real uncomfortable, but said *matter-of-factly*, "Well, when you get married, and you sleep with your husband, you will get pregnant. Then nine months later there's a baby."

"Oh okay, thanks for helping with all this, Sis. I do have this right, don't I? You're saying if I sleep with a man I will get pregnant? Just sleep with him and I don't have to be married to him do I?" I had to get this straight in my head. I knew this was one of those life-changing things.

Ceely rolls her eyes and says, "Yep, I think you got it, but Audie I didn't mean, go to sleep with him. You understand that, don't you? Don't make me go into details. Momma should be talking about this to you, not me." I nodded that I understood, but the thought of all I just heard scares me to death. I also realize why Freddy became a boyfriend to a woman with six kids, or should I say, with daughters?

It's finally, Sunday. *Easter Sunday, and* I'm in my room getting dressed. We are going to see Daddy at Maw Maw's house. I zip up the back of my dress and have a weird feeling that someone was watching me. I look around the room, and then through my mirror, I notice Freddy standing in the door. *Oh my, God,* that door was closed. I didn't even hear him open it. How long has he been there? I spin around at the same time he comes all the way in and shuts the door.

"Hey Audie, your Momma wants to know if you're ready? You're holding everybody up. She said she doesn't want to be gone all day." The whole time he kept staring at me funny. I don't know; he is just acting stranger than normal, and he was talking real low.

"You know Audie, your mother told me you're a woman now, and I think you need someone to show you how a woman should be treated. It's better if it's with someone you know and I will be very gentle with you." With every word he says, the gap between us becomes smaller.

The whole time I'm standing there thinking, *this isn't happening.* I don't know where it came from, but I felt the strength in me I had never felt before.

I gave Freddy the most disgusted look I could muster up and say, "If you come one step closer to me I will scream and remember I am on my way to see my

Daddy. I will tell him, and I don't know what he will do to you, but I do know it won't be good. Oh, and yes Freddy, I am going to tell Momma when I get back."

I wasn't scared. My legs weren't shaking, and my voice sounds strong, but inside I'm thinking, *Freddy will have to kill me before I let him so much as touch a hair on my head.*

Freddy has that nasty grin on his face when he says, "Oh Audie, you're so naïve. Do you think your Mother doesn't know about this already? No that's okay, just run to Mommy and tell her, but don't say I didn't warn you, and I'm not afraid of your Daddy, either."

Before he could say anything else, the door flew open, and it was Cossette. "C'mon Audie, it's taken you forever. Momma says she needs to drop us off and get back here. Oh, Freddy, I didn't see you. What are you doing in our bedroom?" Cossette gave him one of her dirtiest looks.

He just kept that awful grin on his face and tried to pat her on the head. She pushes his hand away as he says, "Well it's none of your business, but I was just telling Audie the same thing you just did."

"Okay, Cossette let's go." As Cossette went out to the door, Earl stops me and says we will discuss this later. I pull away and hurry to catch up with Cossette.

When I return home, Momma is in her room and says she will talk to me tomorrow, because she is tired. I don't see Freddy all night, either. The next day when I get home from school, I talk to Momma. To my surprise, she tells me she knew I was coming to talk to her, and she was hoping I wouldn't.

"Freddy told me you and he had an argument yesterday and that you would probably come to me with something like this, but Audrey, I never expected this of you. You never lie to me, not since you were very young, anyway."

I cut her off, "Momma I'm not lying to you now. It happened just the way I said it did. Don't you see Freddy just told you that so you wouldn't kick him out? He told me you didn't care if he made me a woman. Momma! You have to believe me. Freddy is going to hurt one of us girls. You have to do something, Momma. You have too!" I plead with her; all the while thinking what Ceely will say when I tell her how Momma acted. *I told you so, Audie.*

"That's enough Audrey Rose! You're just making this worse. I'm sorry, but I am going to have to ground you. No talking on the phone and you're not going over to your Grandmothers or Dads for two weeks. Audrey, you know it's talk like this that gets kids taken away from their parents, so I don't want to hear this repeated to no one do you hear?" By then Momma had jerked me out the chair, I was sitting in and told me to go to my room.

Through my tears, I say, "Yeah, sure Momma I guess I do understand, and Momma I never lied to you when I was little, either."

The next day while I was doing dinner dishes, Freddy, walks up behind me and says, "You know *Audie*, I can get you off your grounding if you're nice to me. Of course, you'll have to be *real* nice. Just think about it, and remember I told you so." He laughs and walks away.

I sure the heck didn't want to be grounded and have to be home with him all the time, but he would turn blue and die before I would let him touch me. Carmen moved back home over the weekend from Daddy's.

I ask her what happen to make her come back, "Did you miss me? Oh I know, you missed Momma and Freddy too much to stay away." At the time Brenda left she felt the same way about Freddy as Ceely and I did.

She frowns at me for a minute, and then she smiles and says, "Silly, of course, I missed you, but you know how much love Maw Maw has for Mother and her kids. She didn't want me staying there, *Audie* I don't think she even wants Dad to be there. Let's just leave it at that, okay? I've got to go help mom." She stops and gazes out the window for a second, and then rushes out of the room.

Carmen has changed. She is acting more grown up, and she isn't easy to talk to, anymore. It seems like she spends a lot of time in the bedroom with Momma and Freddy. That isn't unusual for Momma, because if you ever want to talk to her, you have to go to her bedroom. She says that was the only room her and Freddy could find peace and quiet. Momma had a TV in there too, but now she puts a knife in her door to lock it. We used to just walk in, but now we have to knock, and it takes her forever to open it. Sometimes she doesn't, we have to talk to her through the door. I think it is weird too, that Carmen is in there with them now, but if I haven't learned anything else, I know not to question what my Momma does.

Carmen was home two weeks when Daddy came over. Momma met him outside on the porch. At first, they were just talking then Daddy raised his voice.

"Carly, it's not right having *him* live in this house with the girls. The kids have told me some pretty bad things are going on over here. I want him out! What are you thinking letting him be with, Carmen?" Daddy is trying to come in the house.

Freddy walks out to the porch and tells Daddy, *that it will probably be better if he left before they call the police.* How dare he talk to my Daddy like that and what is he saying, *call the police*?

What does Carmen have to do with Freddy? He made a big mistake telling Daddy to leave. Daddy jumps past Momma and hit Freddy. His body flies across the porch and hits the door. Carmen is screaming. Freddy tells Daddy if he doesn't leave he is going to get his gun. Freddy always threatens to use his gun on Daddy, but never threatened Daddy to his face, until now. That's how Freddy is, big talk, but no action and even I know what a coward he was. Momma calmed down and told Freddy to go in the house.

Daddy yells at Freddy, "Yeah, you go call the police and get your gun. Let's see who they will believe when I tell them what my wife has let you do to my daughter!" That stops Freddy in his tracks. He starts talking real nice to Daddy.

"Now Cameron, I don't know what these kids have told you, but nothing is going on here. Did Carmen tell you this stuff? She's just mad because Carly made her break up with her boyfriend a while back." Momma told Freddy just to go in the house. He listened this time and went in, but not before making all of us go in with him.

Momma and Daddy talks a little while longer and then Daddy left. When she comes in, her and Freddy go into the kitchen. I follow Carmen to our bedroom and ask her what just happened.

"Carmen, what was Daddy talking about? What's going on?" I didn't have a clue what was wrong.

Carmen sounded so tired when she answered me, "Audie, I don't know. You're too young to get involved with any of this.

Just go to bed, okay?" She turns, and walks into the bathroom. I could hear her crying.

All I could think of was, *what has happened to my big sister?* I knew I had lost her somewhere along the way. I just didn't know when or where. I decided I was going to talk to Momma, but I stopped when I got close to the kitchen and hear what Freddy is saying to her.

"I'm warning you, Carly; you better keep him away from me. He is insane and because of that he could kill me, and get away with it. Don't make me have to shoot him." I could tell Freddy was trying not to raise his voice.

"Just calm down, he isn't going to kill you. If there's one thing I know about Cameron, he's not a killer. Believe me; I would have been dead a long time ago. Freddy, I still have some control over him. I will talk to him. I will get another restraining order against him if I have to." It sounds like to me; she can control Freddy, too.

Just as I was about to go back to my bedroom, Momma walks out of the kitchen. She scares me so bad, I jump. "Audrey Rose, what are you doing out here? You were told to go to bed."

"I was coming to talk to you, Momma. What's happening? Why is Daddy so mad? Momma, I'm scared." I'm starting to shake.

Freddy walks up to me and says, "It's because of your crazy Daddy. You should be afraid of him."

I saw red at that minute. I had never talked back to an adult, but you don't talk bad about my Daddy. I knew he was crazy sometimes, but he is my Daddy.

"Don't you ever talk about my Daddy that way. You have no right. You're the one that's crazy." I thought he was going to hit me.

He got right in my face and said, "I can say anything I want to. It's none of your *damn business* what goes on in this house. All you kids are spoiled. Carly, you had better get control of her before I do something she will be sorry for! By the way, this is my house if you don't like it leave." I was shaking by then. Why was Momma just standing there? Why didn't she say something?

"Freddy! That's enough. Audrey, you tell Freddy your sorry, and then go to bed. I can't believe you are talking like this. It isn't like you at all. You sound like your sister Ceely? Well, I won't put up with it with her, and I'm not going to with you. Just go to bed I've got a headache." The same thought was going through my head; I can't believe I said anything either, but one thing I know for sure I'm not going to tell that man I'm sorry!

"Momma just one more thing. It isn't Freddy's house. You're the one that works and pays for it. He doesn't even work anymore, and he's not my Daddy he can't tell me what to do." I don't care what happens to me. I'm not going to let him treat us like this.

Freddy started toward me again, but Momma put her hand up. "Your wrong, as long as you're under this roof you will treat him with respect. Yes, Audrey, this is his house, too. It's his and mine. Now get out of my sight."

Lying on my bed, I know there will be no sleep for me tonight until Ceely gets home. I hope she's having fun. When she left earlier with her new boyfriend, she looked happy. Ceely and Levi broke up; I don't know why. I sure miss having Levi around. I could always count on him to make me laugh. I'm not sure about this new guy she's dating. She doesn't bring him around much. Not that I blame her.

I did learn a couple of things tonight. My Momma lied to us; after she had made Daddy leave, she said she would never put a man before us kids, again. Well, tonight she proved that wasn't true. Freddy was also giving me another warning, in his sly way, tonight. My Momma will go along with anything he wanted. I didn't want to believe it before, but now I have, too. I know I can never go to Momma for protection from him, but I know for sure whom I can go to, *my Daddy*. I know now that Freddy is afraid of my Daddy because after all, he is insane. I never dreamed that Daddy's sickness would someday be a form of protection for me. *Yes, God works in mysterious ways.* I don't know why that came into my head, but it did. I haven't thought about God much since Daddy left. Maybe he's trying to tell me something.

It seems like Ceely is never gonna get home. Thank goodness tomorrow is Saturday. Just as I'm drifting off, Ceely comes in; she is so pretty. I wish I looked like Ceely. All the boy's like her. She has the most beautiful hair, thick like Mommas. It is real long and almost black, the color of Daddy's. I would watch her sometimes when she got ready to go out. It never took her long. She doesn't need makeup. Sometimes though she will roll her hair with coke cans, now that looked funny, her hair always curls just right. She reminded me of *Marlo Thomas* the actress on the show 'That Girl', except Donna was prettier.

When she sat down on the bed, I turned to her. "Ceely, how was your date? Did you have fun?" I love to hear about where she would go when she went out.

"Yeah it was fun, just getting away from here is the fun part. We went to a party at this real big house. I guess you could call it a mansion." She is still just sitting on the side of the bed. We all know her new boyfriends' parents are rich. Of course rich to us was if you had a new car, and owned your home.

"Ceely, some bad stuff happened here tonight. Daddy came over and got into a fight with Freddy." Now, she was listening to me. She turns around and stretches out on the bed with her head propped on her hand.

"Really? Why? What did Freddy do or better yet what did Daddy find out?" Her eyes had a sparkle to them.

I looked at her puzzled, so Ceely knows something, too. Why doesn't anybody ever tell me anything? I tell her what has happened. Then I tell her about how Momma let Freddy talk to me. She asked *why that surprised me*, as I knew she would. Ceely said Freddy talks like that to her all the time, and she doesn't take it from him, either. She says it surprises her how blind I can be when it comes to Momma. I tell her, *I guess I just don't want to think of my Momma like I do Freddy*. He can convince Momma of things, just like our Daddy could.

"I know, Momma says I sound like you, and she didn't like it. Ceely, why don't I know a lot of this stuff is happening? I know Freddy talks dirty to us, but I have never heard him talk the way he did tonight to any of us." Donna was looking at me like she knew a lot more than me, which apparently she did.

"There's a lot you younger kids don't hear, Audie. I know, don't look at me like that. You're just 17 months younger than me, but you look a lot younger than that, so people think you're younger than what you are. I bet Freddy sees you in a different light now, but I don't think that is a good thing. You should have stayed quiet, Audie." She looks worried for me.

"Why Ceely, Freddy can't hurt us, and believe me he has already noticed me. I'm not afraid of him, though." I told her what he had said to me on Easter, and that I knew he was afraid of Daddy.

"Yeah, I know I figured out a long time ago why he is afraid of Daddy. Audie, I'm gonna tell you some stuff for your protection. I guess you're old enough to know now." She had my attention, now.

"Freddy is really bad Audie, and so is *Momma*. She let him do some bad things to Carmen. I don't know why Carmen let him, but she did. I don't think she had much of a choice. He tried with me too, but I fought him, and I also told him I would tell Momma if he didn't leave me alone. He told me to go ahead and tell her. She knew what he was doing, and it was okay with her. So I told Momma, and Audie she didn't care. Stay away from him, Audie. He's dangerous, more than Daddy ever was. Promise me you will tell me if he comes near you again? Promise me Audie!" Ceely had tears in her eyes.

"Okay I will, but Ceely what exactly did Momma let him do to Brenda?" I didn't have a clue what she was saying. I knew it was bad, but I wasn't sure what she meant.

"Oh Audie, you know. He touched her in places he shouldn't have and made her do things to him, okay. That's all I'm saying." She turned over and said goodnight.

All I can think of is when I was nine, and I told Momma, Daddy had touched me in places. I knew I had told her that because I was afraid and embarrassed to tell her what he had done. Is that what Ceely is trying to tell me? Freddy did that to Carmen and Momma let him? *Oh God, don't let it be true.* Please don't let it be true. I cried myself to sleep that night and said a prayer of thanks to God for letting me know Freddy is afraid of my Daddy. I know that's all I have, and I ask him to protect us from Freddy.

Chapter 11

"Your dreams have been shattered. They're torn to shreds. You now face a reality of darkness and dread. Your shades of gray have now turned to black. You can only go forward without, looking back."

My seventh grade year has been pretty cool. My school here in Pleasant Grove isn't considered an Elementary School, but it isn't a Junior High either. They call it a Middle School. It goes from Fifth through Seventh grade. I guess the Junior High School had gotten overcrowded, so they made these new schools. I was looking forward to going to Junior High, though, but this school turned out to be pretty good. At the end of school, which will be in a couple of months, we get to have a real Graduation Ceremony with Caps and Gowns. We also get to have a dance. All the girls are excited about it, but the guys are acting like it's no big deal. Two of my girlfriends are going to the dance with boys. They say *you're not considered cool unless you do.*

I told them, as we were walking to class today, "Then I guess I'm not cool, cause I'm not going with no boy anywhere.

Lora made a face at me and said, "Audie, you have too. You don't want to be left out, or made to feel different do you?"

I didn't want to tell her that I was different. None of my friends at school knew me outside of school. They didn't know me at all. I made sure I never got close to anyone. How can I tell them they can't come to my house? How can I explain Freddy, to them? I'm so afraid he might say, or do something to embarrass me, or worse to them. I used to think Momma was so unfair, but now I'm glad she had that rule. I'm ashamed to say this, but I am embarrassed by the way we have to live. That's why I try never to get close to anyone.

Jasmin was different; she seemed to know without me telling her that she isn't welcome at my house. In all the years I have known Jasmin, she never once asked to come over. I always spent the night with her, or she would spend the night with me at my Grandmother's house. I was never ashamed of my Daddy, though. If we were allowed; when Daddy lived with us, I would have brought friends home to meet him. I got so good at reading Daddy's moods, I could tell by the look in his eyes what kind of day we were in store for, so when Daddy had a good day he was fun. I knew my friends would like him, but I also never would forget just how sick he was, either. Freddy has a different kind of sickness one that no doctor can fix. I wasn't going to take a chance, and bring a friend home with him in the house. I'm different all right, in more ways than my friends at school will ever know.

By the time we reach our classroom Lora has already figured out who I should take to the dance. "Audie, he would be perfect for you. Y'all are so cute together anyway, even if you are just studying partners. I know if you ask he will go with you." She says this all in one breath.

Lora was like that. She talks as if it were the last thing she will ever be able to say. She has this real *southern drawl* too. The boys just love her.

"Lora, slow down. Who are you talking about? Surely! Not Luke? Oh no! I'm not going to ask Luke. I'm not asking anybody. Besides the boy is supposed to ask a girl, not the other way around. This girl asks boy thing is silly. Lora, Luke and I are just friends; that's all." I was looking at her as if she had lost her mind.

I sat down at my desk and opened my History Book to the chapter on the *Civil War*. I can't concentrate on what I'm reading, for thinking about what Lora said as she walked away.

"We will talk about this later, Audie. Maybe, just maybe, I will drop a hint in Luke's *little ole' ear*." I told her if she did I would never speak to her again.

Hearing, Mrs. Rogers, our teacher calling for attention in the class broke my train of thought.

"Okay, class get into your groups and work on your projects while I grade papers."

The sound of a desk scratching across the floor made me turn. Steve is dragging his desk over to mine. Our project is to make a notebook on the *Civil War*. We are making maps of all the battles fought and writing essays on the Generals and their armies. In conclusion, we are making a list of the effects the *Civil War* had on the North and South. This assignment will be half of our semester grade, so Luke and I are taking it very seriously. I'm writing the essay's because writing is my strong point and I love doing research. Luke is drawing the maps. Luke, could be an artist because that's what he is really good doing. He could be an artist, but his dream is to be an architect. One thing is for certain, neither one of us wants to be anything more than friends.

Carmen, once told me, *never date a friend, Audie, because if something happens and you brake up, you will lose him as a friend forever.* I've never dated anybody, and I don't plan on it, now. From what I can tell by watching Carmen, and Ceely you get your heart broken. I don't plan on dating at all. Well, maybe when I'm 18, but I'm not sure about that either. Besides, no one will want to date me. I overheard Momma and Aunt Jean talking once, and Aunt Jean said I would probably have trouble getting boyfriends. Momma said she was probably right. I knew they were talking about my scars. I decided right then if all a boy wants me for is how I look on the outside then I didn't need him. Yeah, at twelve I can be real brave. Who needs boys? My heart was hurting. No, I would never ask Luke to take me to the dance. I can go alone, if I go at all.

After History, we have P.E. Oh, how I hate this class. We have to change into our white starchy gym suit. Then at the end of class, we have to take a shower before getting dressed, this is the part I hate. Most of the time I will take as long as I can to get undressed; until I was sure every girl had left the locker area, before getting into the shower. Sometimes I'm able to fake the teacher out and make her think I showered, but not today. Walking out of the shower area I see her standing by the door inspecting all of us as we leave. I hear her heavy footsteps come up to my dressing area.

Breathing heavily she says, "Addison, are you gonna make a career out this?"

"No Ms. Sparks, I'm almost done. That time of the month you know. I will hurry." She makes me nervous. I was praying that she would walk away.

"Well you better hurry, or you're going to be late, and I'm not writing you a note. So get a move on." *All she needs is a whip*, I thought to myself.

I wrap my towel around me and peek out of the Curtin. Yea, she was gone. Just as I get to where the showers are Ms. Sparks walks up. She scares me so bad I dropped my towel. Oh no, I hurried to wrap it back around me.

I hear her gasp, and then see her look down at the floor as she says, "Uh, I'm sorry I thought you were through. I didn't mean to startle you. Uh, hurry up okay. Hey, I will write you a note. Stop by my office on the way out."

That was uncomfortable. Darn, should I try to explain to Ms. Sparks what happened to me, or just let it go? I know she has seen the scars on my legs, because of my gym shorts. Oh well, guess I better say something. I don't want her to be nervous around me. That's why I try not to let my scars show. I hate to make people nervous. My family is used to seeing them, so I sometimes forget how people might react.

When I walked into her office she seems to be moving papers around on her desk, "Ms. Sparks, I'm sorry about what happened back there. When I was three, I got burned. That's why it always takes me so long in the showers. I try to wait until everyone is done." I had been looking at the floor while talking.

When I look up, she is waving at me to stop. She looks like she is gonna cry when she says, "Audrey, no it's me who should apologize. I'm so sorry for walking in on you. I thought you were going to try and get out of taking a shower, again. Yes, I know all you girls try, but if you had come to me, I would have made an allowance for you. You know you have a very good reason not too. From here on out you don't have to take a shower if you don't want too. I just wish you would have come to me before this."

"Thank you Ms. Sparks, but it wouldn't be fair to the other students if I did that, besides they would notice. How will I explain it to them?" I was feeling nervous. She's never been a teacher I thought I could talk too, especially about this.

"Since I'm the teacher, I think I make the decisions around here; besides you brought me a doctors note. It's really sad that you have to use a special soap on your skin so it won't dry out. As of tomorrow no more showers for you, Addison. Now here's your tardy note and get to class." That's the teacher I know. She always calls us by our last name.

"Thanks, see you tomorrow." I didn't wait another second. I grabbed the note and practically ran out of her office.

When I got to Study Hall, I gave the teacher my note and sat down. I could see Lora was excited about something. She almost didn't wait for me to sit down before she starts talking.

"Got some really good news for Y'all. Guess what certain boy is waiting to be asked to the dance by a certain girl?" She looks like *the cat that had swallowed the canary*, as my grandmother always says.

"Lora, you had better be talking about some other girl and boy we know. Oh Lora, tell me you didn't!" I just couldn't take any more embarrassment today.

"Oh, don't be silly, of course, it's Y'all. It wasn't hard at all. After P.E., by the way, where did you disappear too? Oh never mind tell me later. I went and waited for Luke to come out of the boy's gym. He's slow too, but I asked him if he was taking anybody to the dance. That silly boy asked me what dance. Of course, I reminded him, and he said he didn't know if he was going. So then I ...," Just then the teacher said we would get a detention if we didn't stop talking. She moved Lora up front by her desk.

As she was picking up her books, Lora whispers, "Wait for me after class, okay?"

The teacher told her very sternly to get up front now.

I nodded at her. I couldn't get a detention. Momma will kill me. Besides, I have never had one before, and I don't want to start now. Oh great, she didn't finish telling me what Luke had said. Oh well, I can never face him now. I won't go. I'll just tell him I can't go. Darn, I'll have to think of something good to tell him. I sit for the rest of the period thinking. Out of all the girls in this school, how did I become friends with Lora, we are so different in every way. When the bell rang, Lora couldn't get to my desk fast enough.

"Boy, I'm glad this day is over. Lora call me tonight and tell me what you said to Luke so I can get us both out of this silly plan of yours. I can't hang around and talk, I've got to get home." I was trying to hurry so I could leave the school before Luke see's me. I should have known Lora isn't going for that.

"No just walk to my locker and I will walk home with you. It won't take but a minute. I can't wait until later and besides, after all I went through for you and Luke to go together your not getting out of it." She sounds like she was upset with me.

"Lora this isn't my fault. I ask you not to do this. Besides, he probably won't go. C'mon lets go to your locker, and you can walk part of the way home with me. I can't have anyone over after school without getting permission first." She was already talking to one of her other friends. I picked up my books and followed.

Once we were away from the school, she gave me the whole scoop, as she called it. "Well, I say to Luke he needs to go to the dance, cause all the seventh grade class is going, afterall, the dance is for our graduation. I told him there was one *teeny* more problem; he needed to be invited by a girl. That threw him, but after I got through convincing him to go I innocently asked him who he thought he would like to go with. Of course, he said he didn't know. Then I told him you wanted to go, but you didn't know who to ask." I could have strangled her right then and there.

"You didn't tell him that. Lora that isn't true."

She cut me off. "Oh shush, and let me finish. I told Luke you are my best friend, and I would just die if you decided not to go, so he said he would go with you, but he didn't think you will want to go with him." Her eyes were dancing around like someone just told her she was going to Disneyland.

"Did he say that? I mean that I wouldn't want to go with him? Oh, he's right I don't want to go, not now." What was I thinking he only agreed to ask me because she tricked him into it?

"Okay Audrey Rose, we've got to part ways here but promise me you will at least think about it. I don't want to go without you, and neither does Shelly, okay?" She smiled and waved goodbye.

The next day in Mrs. Smith's class it happens. Luke brought up the dance. I could tell he seems uncomfortable every time he talks to me and so do I. Then finally while we were working on our History folder he asked.

"I hear we are going to have an end of the year dance. I was uh, wondering are you going with anybody. I mean did you ask anybody yet. Well, if you haven't I was wondering if you would, uh think about maybe asking me?" His voice sounded higher than usual, and I was looking at him like I would rather be anywhere but here.

"Well no, I haven't asked anyone yet. I was thinking about not going. Okay Luke, will you go with me, but only as friends, okay? My Momma doesn't let me date yet. Besides, you're my friend and study partner. I think we probably can have fun." In my head I was thinking, *oh shut up Audrey, you sound like an idiot.*

"Well sure that's what I was thinking, just as friends. I'm sorry, I didn't mean for you to think we were anything else." Now he sounded like an *idiot.*

"Okay, then we'll just meet there. Did you get those maps finished? Mrs. Rogers wants us to let her see what we have so far next week, and it would look better if we had at least a couple of maps in here." Control, I had to get things back in control, and it worked.

"Oh yeah, here what do you think of these. I will have some more on Monday, okay?" I breathe a sigh of relief. My friend Luke is back, and his voice is back to normal, I too.

The rest of the school year just flew. Luke and I got an A on our Civil War notebook. Matter of fact, Mrs. Smith asked if she could keep it as an example for her students next year. We were both proud to let her. Besides, I've learned a lot about people in History from her. This class made me realize how important it is to know about *family history*, and where we come from is important. Graduation came and went. We all walked across the stage and got our Diplomas. I felt sad that the year was over. I think this was probably my best year of school. I got to go to the same school all year, from beginning to end.

I'm on my way to the dance, and I feel excited. It surprises me because I tried real hard not to be. Momma bought me a new dress. It's yellow with a fine wisp of lace covering it. Ceely did my hair. She put it up on top of my head with little flowers and butterflies in it. I felt like Cinderella going to the ball. Driving up in front of the school, I immediately see Lora and Shelly with their dates. Momma says to meet her here when the dance is over. I tell her I will and jump out of the car.

Lora squeals and runs over to me. "Oh, look at you. You're just beautiful. Why Miss Addison, if I didn't know you better I would think you were dressed to meet a beau. I'm so glad you came after all." She could be so funny when she wants too, and I am embarrassed.

"C'mon let's go in. Have Y'all seen Luke?" We were almost to the gym when I realized they have stopped walking.

"Audrey, Luke didn't tell you? I mean he didn't call?" I shook my head and asked her why he would call?

"Is Luke not coming? Did something happen?" I'm confused cause they looked nervous.

"Well, oh darn this is all my fault. Audie, he's here, but he came with that new girl, Cynthia. I thought you knew. When I saw them get out of his Dad's car, I went over to them. I ask him why he was with her, and not you. He said you didn't mind cause y'all are just friends. I'm sorry; I thought you knew." A car could have hit me at that moment, and I wouldn't have felt a thing.

I knew I couldn't show it, though, so I got control of myself and said, "It's okay Lora. He's right; we are just friends. Yeah, it would have been nice if he told me. Then I wouldn't have had to come to this stupid dance, but hey let's go inside and have fun."

"Oh, you're such a trooper, Audrey. He is going to be so jealous when he see's you looking like you do. He will be sorry he brought, her!" Lora was back to her giddy self.

The gym looks nice. It is decorated like outer space. Thank goodness it's dark up there in space. I don't think I can keep this fake smile on my face much longer. I wish the floor would just swallow me up. If I could, I would have run home as quick as I could, but I'm not going to. I guess you call it pride or just plain stubbornness. I knew I was going to stick it out as long as I could. Shelly and Lora keep trying to get their dates to dance with me. Of course, they didn't want to. They barely wanted to dance with them. Lora keeps dragging hers out to the dance floor. Now I know how a *wildflower* feels, this will be the first and last time I ever get myself in this position. After about an hour I call Momma and ask her to get me. I tell her it's boring, and I'm ready to come home. Just as I get to the door of the gym, I bump into Luke, with Cynthia holding on to him.

"Oh hi, Audrey you look nice. Are you having fun? It's cool how they set this up, huh?" Luke says looking everywhere, except at me.

"Hi, yes it's nice, but I have to go. My Momma said I could only stay an hour. Y'all

-174-

have fun; bye gotta go." I was trying real hard to get away.

But not before Cynthia says, "Oh we will, bye." Luke takes her arm and is trying to pull her across the room.

Watching them, I realize how much I had wanted to to be at this dance with Luke. Well, maybe it wasn't Luke, but the excitement of going with a boy somewhere. I guess on a date. No matter what I call it, it would have been a date. Shaking my head I put on my best smile, all the while dreading having to pretend any longer that I am having a good time. *Oh Momma, hurry up and get here.*

Momma didn't know I was meeting a boy here. Surprisingly, she is very strict with me when it comes to boys. I guess she thinks I need protection from them. Little does she know the wolf is right under her roof, or maybe she did, at this point, I didn't care. Ceely and Carmen are the only one's that knew about Luke.

All the way home Momma wanted to know all about the dance. With a stern look, she asked me if I danced with anyone.

"No Momma, I don't think boys my age like to dance. Most of them stood around talking, and acting stupid like boys do. I had fun with my girlfriends, though. I'm glad I went. Thanks for letting me go.

"Well hon, you're right boys are like that at this age, but there will come a time when they start noticing girls."

Momma, is Ceely still up?" I want to change the subject. Momma is asking too many questions.

"As a matter of fact she is, so is Carmen. I guess you want to talk to them, huh?"

"Yeah, my sisters worked hard to get me ready. I want to share with them how it went."

Running into the house; I see Carmen first. I tell her how much fun I had. I don't say anything about how awful my night was. I find Ceely in our bedroom. Finally, how I feel spills out all over my face.

Donna lets me cry for a few minutes and then says sarcastically, "Boy's can be insensitive pigs, *sis*. That's just how they are, Audie. They don't think like we do. He probably doesn't even realize he hurt you. Remember you did tell him you only wanted to go as *friends*. Not that it makes it right what he did. He should have at least called you." She's trying hard to say the right things to me. I know she wanted to kick him in his rear.

"Yeah, your right Ceely, but it still hurts." Ceely is the only one I can talk about private stuff. She always understands how I feel. I bet no boy would ever dump Ceely for someone else.

Well, this is why I will not date until I'm at least 18. Carmen is right. I lost a friend tonight. Boys stink! I'm glad schools out for the summer. I don't think I can face Luke anytime soon, maybe never! Besides I had enough on my hands trying to stay out of Freddy's reach.

A week after the dance Momma says we are moving back to *Oak Cliff*. I guess we've been in one place too long, or maybe we can't afford this house anymore; after all, Momma quit working. I didn't know when it happened, but a couple of weeks ago I noticed Momma started being home all the time. I don't know how we pay for anything cause Freddy doesn't work either. Oh great, now they will both be home all summer. I have a feeling things are fixing to get a lot tougher around here.

Chapter 12

"A child cries from hunger; a mother stops the pain.
An abused child cries to be saved; a mother turns
away.
A child cries to be held; a mother opens her arms.
An abused child cries to be loved; a mother closes
her heart."

Well, we're back in Oak Cliff again. I am attending Boude Story Junior High for my eighth-grade year. I'm not happy because I don't know anyone. It's so different from last year. This school seems so big, and everyone has their group of friends that they hang around. Every class I go to has a different teacher and different students. The only good thing about it is Ceely goes here too. She's in the ninth grade. I don't think I will ever make a friend here. I'm just too shy I guess. Oh well, it's better than being home all the time. My summer at home consisted of avoiding Freddy as much as I could. He seemed to be getting braver in the disgusting things he would say and do to us.

One beautiful Thursday morning I was lying on my bed writing in my diary and listening to the birds sing outside my window. Every morning the first thing I did, after getting the kids up and dressed, would be to open my window and let the new day come in. I couldn't stand to be closed in. Since I was a little girl, I would just panic if my face gets covered with something. I can't even stand to have a towel thrown over my head when someone is drying my hair. I know now it's called Claustrophobia. Whatever they want to call it I don't care. All I know is I feel like I'm in a coffin with no way out, so needless to say I don't like darkness in my life of any kind, physically or mentally.

Concentrating hard on what I'm writing, I don't hear the bedroom door open, and Freddy walk in. He is why I spend as much time as I can in my room reading or writing, to block out of my life what's on the other side of that door. When he gets near my bed, I jump, because he has thrown something down in front of me on the bed. It appears to be a Polaroid picture that has landed face down on my pillow.

I look up at him and ask, "Freddy, what is this?" I reach over to pick up the picture but stop to ask, "Does Momma want me for something?"

Freddy has that sneering grin on his face and winks at me, "No Audie; I need you to do something. Pick up that picture and take a look at what you're missing by playing hard to get."

I rose up on one elbow, and a long sigh turned it over. Gosh, I wish Freddy would leave me alone. My next words caught in my throat as my eyes and attention focused on the picture. I thought I would vomit when I realize what I'm seeing. I can't speak or move. It's as if time froze, and the picture is glued to my hand. I drop it as if it were burning my fingers and jump off my bed. It is a Polaroid picture of Freddy in the *nude* holding his private part in his hand grinning. With my hand over my mouth, I run to the bathroom to throw-up. My brain won't let me. I just keep gagging until there were tears in my eyes. After what seems like forever I stop and wet a rag to wash my face. I get the bar of Ivory soap and scrub my hands. I feel so dirty. Where's Momma I've got to find her? He's gone too far this time! I slowly open the bathroom door and look out. Freddy is nowhere in sight. I say a quiet prayer of thanks to *God*. I go to the Kitchen no one is there. The backyard is empty too. The TV is on, but no one is watching it. Where is everyone? *Please, don't tell me I'm alone with him.* I quietly walk back down the hall toward the boy's bedroom. I have to pass the room Momma, and Freddy sleep in. I'm afraid he is in there. I get to the door and remember Junior went to live with Daddy last weekend so he wouldn't be here, but Cossette and Craig are here somewhere. I open the door, and ever so quietly call for Cossette. No answer and the room is empty. I knew Momma and Carmen are at the store, and Ceely is working. Where are the kids? I was starting to feel trapped. Freddy had never forced himself on me before, so I didn't think he would now, but he has never done anything as horrific as this to me before, neither. My legs are feeling weak with fear. I try to calm down. I decide to sit on the front porch until someone comes home. Just as I tip toe past Momma's room, the door fly's open and Freddy pulls me inside and slams it. A scream catches in my throat. He has me by my waist. He is so close I can smell his cologne. It makes my stomach turn. To this day I get sick every time I smell Old Spice cologne on anyone. My mind is racing a mile a minute on how to get away from him when a movie I have seen pops into my head. I raise my right foot and bring it down hard on his. That did it he let go of me, and I fell to the ground. Jumping up and run for the door. Just as I thought I was free, he throws himself in front of the door to block me.

Freddy is a tall man, maybe six foot. With wavy reddish blond hair styled for the 1940's. He is very, very skinny. He had deep brown freckles covering his face and body. When he opens his mouth, it seems his teeth were too big to fit inside. I think his eyes were brown or maybe green. I can't remember ever looking into them long enough to know the color exactly. I was afraid too. Afraid of what I might see.

I fall into his body as we both hit the door. I push away and slowly look up. He is looking down at me with this terrifying grin on his face and says, "Awe, you're a little spitfire aren't you Audie? I like my women that way. Now calm down I'm not going to make you do anything you don't want to do. Come over here; I just want to talk to you" He had locked the door and was sitting on the bed. The lock on the door was a bolt lock, and it was too high for me to reach.

"Freddy if you don't let me out right now I'm going to start screaming." I'm trembling, and my voice is shaking. I don't think I have ever been this scared, and I've been pretty scared before.

He got a serious look on his face and says, "Just who do you think will hear you? No one is home. I ask your Mother to take the kids with her. You think she doesn't know what my plans are?"

Now I was mad. Freddy is lying. "Freddy, there's no way my Momma knows about this. No way. I know there are some thing's she lets you get away with, but not this. Not with me! Freddy, all I'm telling you is you better let me out or kill me, cause I will tell someone and you will go to Jail. Daddy will kill you if I tell him and you know it!" He got that stupid grin on his face again and started walking toward me.

I was pressed against the wall by the door when he finally says, "I'm going to let you out, not because I'm afraid of your Daddy, but because I don't have to force anyone to get what I want. You will come around sooner or later Audie. They always do." He reaches toward me, and I flinch.

Freddy runs his hand up my arm and then away from me, and I hear the door unlock.

Just as I reach for the doorknob, he says, "Audie, if you would just let me love you one time you will come begging for more. You saw the picture."

I push past him and run outside. I don't stop until I'm down the block. I stop at the corner and look around, not realizing where I am, just that I had to get away. I see the church across the street. There is a line of bushes with pretty white and yellow flowers hiding the front porch of the church. I run across the street and up the steps to the porch. Slowly I sink to the floor. I lower my head to my knees and wrap my arms around them, so I can make myself as small as possible. I feel the coolness of the wood planks penetrating the thin material of my shorts. I'm tired. I fee like I have just run from the *Devil* himself. What am I going to do? How do I save myself, much less my little brother and sister? I tell myself to pray. Audrey pray, so I did.

For some reason, a lady we had studied about in Mrs. Rogers's seventh grade class came to mind. Her name was Rosa Parks; she was a 42-year-old black seamstress from Montgomery, Alabama. Mrs. Rogers had us study her and the effects of her refusal to give up her seat to a white man on a city bus, in 1955. She had wanted us to see how far the Black American race had come since slavery and the people who were brave enough to stand up for what they believe. It was because of Rosa Parks's brave decision that day that Martin Luther King Jr.; another brave Black American, was able to bring The Civil-Rights Act into a full movement. Rosa Parks and Martin Luther King won their fight too; on December 21, 1956, the Montgomery Transit System was integrated. Martin Luther King fought right along side of this brave woman for all black people to have equal rights. President Kenedy tried, too. Daddy once told me he thinks this is why the president died, because of *his loyalty to certain people's civil rights.* One thing I did gain from my journey with Rosa Parks is the strength it must have taken her to stand up to that man on the bus and then to our* *Nation.* My next thought is if one little woman can do that, then surely I can stand up and fight Freddy. If only I had someone like Martin Luther King Jr. to stand by me. That someone should be my Mother, but I knew by now Momma wasn't going to save us. I knew Momma would stand by Freddy not me. There was something else I knew, and it scared me to death. I would rather fight the Nation than my Momma!

I knew what I had to do even if she didn't believe me, because if I didn't, I would lose myself forever. I felt some strength coming back to me. Another thought worked it's way into my 13-year-old brain. I knew Jesus was with me; for some reason, I knew He would never abandon me. Jesus would always be there to save me from losing my mind and soul; that was a promise from him that lived within my heart. I also knew that it would have to be a living breathing person to protect me physically. I just didn't know who that would be.

When I finally got the courage to go home, Momma was back. Carmen and Momma are getting the groceries out of the back of the car. I don't see Freddy's car in the driveway. I walk into the kitchen and look out the back door. Cossette and Craig are in the back yard playing. They look happy; Momma has bought them some candy at the store. I remember when getting a piece of candy was the highlight of my day, and I thought it could cure all my unhappiness just by eating it. Carmen walks into the kitchen with two bags in her hand. She looks tired, so I take a bag from her and star putting things away. Carmen was 15 almost 16, but she looks much older. She doesn't even try now to fix herself up, and she's never dated again after David. Something was wrong, but I didn't know what. She just looked so empty. I realize I have calmed down. I wasn't scared anymore, just sick at my stomach. The unfairness of our situation was sitting in again. I shouldn't have to worry about Stuff like this, but most of all I didn't want to talk to Momma about it, so I decided to talk to Ceely. I had a feeling that it wouldn't do any good to talk to Carmen. I would just have to wait until Ceely gets home.

I did ask Carmen how was it that Momma could afford to buy groceries and pay rent when she wasn't working? "Well Audrey, you know Momma is on Welfare. It helps from the State."

"Yeah, I know what Welfare is Carnen, but I thought they only give Food Commodities. Don't we have to go pick the food up from that big warehouse anymore? I always hate going to get food from that Government food place; it takes all day. There are many women with little kids. I do feel sorry for the kids to have to hang around that place so long," for some reason I never thought that I was in the same shape as those kids.

Brenda laughed, it was good to see her laugh. She gave me a little shove and said, "Little sister, sometimes you amaze me with the things you say. No, we don't have to do that anymore. The *State* has a thing called a *Food Stamp System* now. They give you this booklet what that looks like paper money inside, and you take them to the store and spend them like cash, but you can only buy food. You can't buy anything that the Government has put a tax on."

"Gosh, when did you get so smart? It sounds kind of like *Monopoly* money, so how does she pay the rent? Does the *State* help with that too? I know she's not paying other *Bills*. There was a Loan Company called the other day for the hundredth time and she made me tell them again she wasn't here. I hate to lie, Carmen. They don't believe me. The man on the phone got really rude and said he knew I was lying and tell Momma they were going to come and take the TV if she didn't call him back." I didn't realize Brenda has stopped putting things away and was looking at me until she dropped the can she was holding.

Just as I turn, I see tears in her eyes. She bends down to pick up the can and says, "Sis, how am I supposed to know where our mother gets her money? I don't know; you'll have to ask her all these questions. I am sorry you have to answer the phone and talk to those people, just call me next time and I will, okay? Audie, will you finish I have to go to the bathroom." With that said she rushes out of the kitchen.

I can't talk to Carmen lately. It's like when I complain or ask her something about Momma she feels I'm attacking her too. Oh, I just don't know what's up with her. I turn to finish putting the can goods away. With every can I slam down, I see Freddy's face with that *snide grin. Why doesn't he just go away?* Better yet *why doesn't my Momma make him leave?* Just as I slam the cabinet door, Ceely walks in.

"Hey Audie, are you trying to break those cans open the hard way? Why don't you use a can opener?" She looked pretty and sophisticated.

Her job is with the Oak Cliff Tribune selling newspaper subscriptions over the phone. Even though Ceely is just 14 she works hard and would always give Momma her check when she gets paid. Momma's theory is *if we are old enough to work then we could help her pay for stuff we needed around the house.* I guess Freddy doesn't fall into the same category as us. Ceely said she doesn't mind, though. It keeps her out of the house.

"Oh Ceely, I'm so glad your home, I need to talk to you, now! C'mon, let's go to our room before *Freddy* gets back." I grab her arm and pull her to the bedroom we share.

"Okay, you talk while I change." She pulls a pair of shorts out of our dresser drawer. "I take it he did something really bad by the look on your face, so just say it and get it over with."

"Ceely, your just not going to believe how awful it was. I'm still sick at my stomach." All the pent up anger I felt has left me like someone has let the air out of me. I was ashamed to speak it out loud as if somehow it was my fault.

Ceely read my thoughts. "Okay sis, take a deep breath and tell me. None of this is our fault, Audie. I can't even imagine why any of this is happening to us, but it is. We only have each other. So start talking!" She had sat down next to me on the bed.

I push myself back and cross my legs. Once I start, I can't stop. It all just poured out of me; even the part at the church and my memory about Rosa Parks. I told her how it gave me strength, but when I got home and saw Momma I chickened out and decided to talk to her first.

"Well to begin with you didn't chicken out. That was God protecting you again. Audie, I'm glad you came to me first because I have to tell you something about Momma, and her relationship with Freddy. What I have to say about them is going to make you; not just sick to your stomach, but all the way through to your bones. I wish I didn't have too, but I know now to protect you I have too." She got up and looked outside the door to make sure no one was coming. She quietly closed the door and bent down on one knee.

I knew what she was doing. She was making sure the toilet paper we had put in the key whole of our bedroom door was firmly in place. We had to do this in our bathroom too because we caught Freddy looking through the keyhole once while we were changing. After she had made sure no one could see or hear us; Ceely crawled to the middle of our bed in front of me. She sat looking down at the pattern on the bed twisting a piece of thread that had come loose on our blanket.

"Freddy showed me that picture too, Kat. Not too long ago. He said Mother knew he was doing it, but the only difference is he ask me if I would have a baby by him. He says our Mother can't have babies, and he wants one. I didn't believe him and told him I was going to tell Momma. It affects me in the same way as it did you, but I never thought he would go this far with you. My God, you still look like a little girl." Ceely covered her mouth and slowly takes a deep breath.

Lowering her hand and with a shallow breath, she says, "Audie, I went to Mother and told her. Audie, she knew. She said she wanted to give Freddy a child and that I wouldn't have to worry they wouldn't tell anyone. We would go away so no one would know. I screamed at her that she is as sick as he is, and I would never let that man touch me much less have his baby!" Ceely looks like she doesn't know if she wanted to be sick or cry. I was crying for her, though. This hurt so bad.

She cleared her throat and continued, "Of course Mother slapped me and called me a few names, but I didn't care, sis. Nothing she did at this point could have hurt me more. I didn't know what to do after that or who to tell. I thought about it for days but kept coming to the same conclusion. There was no one, so I did nothing but held it inside. Maybe that's wrong, but I had nowhere else to turn," She was shaking so I put my arms around her.

I whispered in her ear. "Ceely what are we going to do? How do we stop someone like him?"

"I don't know Audie, but we can protect ourselves. We know for a fact that Freddy is afraid of our Dad, and I would tell Dad, but I don't want to ruin his life any more than it already is. I hate Freddy, but I don't want him to be killed either, especially by our Dad. Freddy's not worth it!" We both sat there for a minute letting everything sink in.

Ceely turned to me and said, "Audie, maybe you should tell Mother what Freddy did? She seems to protect you more. I don't think she knew Freddy was going to do that to you. I've heard our mother tell him to *leave you alone*. That you're too young to understand the things he says and does."

"I guess I should be grateful. For once I'm glad I look younger than what I am. It doesn't matter Ceely he shouldn't be doing this to any of us. Wonder if he tries this with Cossette?" That thought just dawned on me. I think I would kill him myself.

"Oh, he won't. For one thing, Cossette is meaner than any man Freddy has ever come up against, and besides she's too young, he likes them a little older." I thought I was going to be sick all over again at the thought of him hurting my little sister. She was just a baby. I told Ceely this.

"Now you know how I feel about you, Audie. You're still my baby sister too" She leaned over and hugged me. "Okay, I'm going to go help Carmen with dinner. You see if you can catch Momma alone."

"Ceely just a minute. Do you talk to Carmen about any of this?" I was just curious.

"No, it's like Mother and Freddy have turned Carmen away from me. Not that we have ever been close, but we used to talk. I don't know I feel I can't talk to Carmen about any of this." That's what I needed to know, so it wasn't just a feeling I had. I told her I felt the same way.

I walk slowly down the hallway to Mommas' bedroom. Oh, how I dreaded talking to her about this. I think I knew deep inside what she was going to say, and I just didn't want to hear it. I lightly tapped on her door.

I hear her turn down the TV. "Momma, can I come in and talk to you a minute? It's me, Audrey."

"I can tell it's you. I may have half a dozen kids, but I can tell you apart by your voice you know. I'm just kidding with ya, C'mon in." Oh good, she is in a good mood, but won't be for long.

Just as I was opening her door, I caught sight of Ceely out of the corner of my eye. She was waving like crazy to get my attention. I look at her and spread my arms as if to say, what? She is pointing toward the front of the house and shaking her head no.

She came closer and whispered, "Freddy's home he is in there with her. Don't go in."

I nearly jumped out of my skin when the doorknob pulled out of my hand. I turn around, and there stood Freddy. At that moment I think I really could have thrown up with no problem.

He looked at me and then down the hall at Ceely. "What are you two up too? Audrey, you got something to say to your Mother?" Freddy looks past me at Ceely and then shuts the door.

Momma was lying on the bed with a cigarette in her hand. I'm always afraid she is going to fall asleep and catch herself on fire. Just as I open my mouth to speak Ceely throws the door open and comes in.

She looks upset as she says, "Audrey I asked you to come help with the kids. Carmen and I can't get anything done with them under our feet." She gave Freddy a dirty look and then turned to Momma.

"I was trying to get her when Freddy slammed the door in my face!"

"You know never to barge into my room. You need to knock first. Audrey, go on with your sister and help. Unless what you have to say can't wait?" She was looking at me waiting. I could tell she was getting upset with us.

"Uh, no Momma it can wait. I better help. I'll talk to you later. It's just about my new school." I was stumbling over every word. Freddy knew what I wanted to say. Darn, now he was going to tell her a lie and Momma would believe him.

"Girls, tell Carmen to come here, and are you to finished with dinner?" Momma looked at Freddy, and he winked at her.

We left the room as fast as we could. "Oh great Ceely, now what do I do? He knows what I want to talk to Momma about, and now Carmen has to go in there with them. I wonder why?" I'm trying to keep up with Ceely.

She is taking long strides through the hallway like she is mad or something. "What do you think they want with her, and it's not they, it's him! Just watch after Carmen goes in Momma will come out. Like it's normal for her to leave Carmen in there with him and we aren't supposed to notice. God forbid if we question it. Goodness Audrey, don't you notice any of the sick things that happen around here?" We have just entered the kitchen, and Carmen is draining the water from the potatoes she has boiled.

She turned when she heard us, "Oh good, Audie will you sit the table? Ceely, I need you to stir the Goulash, and make some tea." She stops when she see's the look on Ceely's' face.

"No Carmen, we will finish it all. Your presence has been requested in Mommas' room." Ceely said this rudely to her. It upset me. I thought she was too mean to Carmen. It's not her fault.

Carmen seems not to notice the rudeness in Ceely's' voice. She lowers her head and says quietly, "Okay sorry; I'll try to be right back." She looks sad.

I was deep in thought as I sat the table. Ceely's *right I don't notice anything around here. No, it's not that. I do notice I just don't question anything that doesn't seem right.* What did Ceely mean by the sick things that go on around here? NO! I'm not going even to try to imagine why Freddy wants Carmen in Mommas' room or why Momma will let her go. I need to set the table.

Momma entering the dining room snaps me out of my thoughts. Ceely was right, again. "Audrey what was it you wanted to know about your new school?" She sat down at the table and lit a cigarette.

Momma never used to smoke this much. Heck, she just started smoking last year. My mind is racing. *Oh shoot, what do I tell Momma about school.*

"Uh, Momma what I have to talk to you about will take a while. Can we do it after dinner? Just me and you?" My hand shook as I put a fork by one of the plates.

"Yeah I suppose. It will have to be right after dinner, though. I have to get up early and talk to your Dad. He's acting up again, and your Maw Maw can't handle him." She gets up and goes into the kitchen with Ceely.

I hear her telling Ceely she had better keep her dirty looks to herself. She said she saw the look Ceely gave Freddy when she busted into her room, and she wouldn't have it. "Do you want me to send you away Ceely Jo? Is that what you want, because believe me I can. Don't push me, Ceely."

I walk into the kitchen just as Ceely tells Momma she doesn't care. Maybe it would be better to live with strangers than here. Momma raises her hand to hit Ceely.

I drop the silverware I am caring to put back in the drawer, "Oh I'm sorry. Momma, I think I heard Craig crying for you. It sounded like him, and Junior are fighting again."

"I swear Freddy's right. You, kids, are out of control. Hurry and get dinner on the table. I want Y'all in bed early tonight." She spun around and almost ran to Craig's side. I feel bad for telling a lie, but I can't let her hit Ceely. When what Ceely is saying is right.

"Thanks, Audie, but you didn't have to do that. I'm getting used to it. Here put this on the table and tell our warden dinners ready." I could tell Ceely's voice was shaky. Not from fear, but frustration.

"Ceely, please don't make her upset any more than she is. I still have to talk to her tonight." I feel bad for Ceely. She gets the brunt of Momma's anger every time.

After dinner, we got the little ones into bed. Not without a fight, though. They didn't understand why we were putting them to bed so early. Of course, Momma was nowhere in sight to back us up when we told them she wanted them in bed early. Ceely has a date with her new boyfriend, so I do the dishes. When I finish, I go out back to sit on the porch steps. I love how it smells at night so clean and fresh. It is Fall, and there is just a hint of winter in the air. One thing for sure Momma likes things clean, inside and out. Of course, she didn't have to do any of the chores. That's why she had kids, so she likes to remind us. The back door slams and startles me.

Momma sat down beside me and says, "Okay Audrey, I'm all yours. What's on your mind?" She lit a cigarette.

I watch the flame from her lighter flare up in the still night. It illuminated her face. She looks older since she met Freddy, I thought. When did that happen? Momma always looks younger than her age. Maybe it was just the shadows made by the flame. The end of the cigarette got dark red and angry looking as she inhaled. The tip of the cigarette is called a cherry after it is lit. I heard Freddy making a dirty joke about it to Momma and Aunt Jean one day. Comparing it to a part of the woman's anatomy, Yuk!

I take a deep breath and start, "Momma Freddy did something terrible to me today while you were gone to the store. No Momma, don't roll your eyes. Just let me get it all out before you say anything, okay? Momma, telling you this is hard for me." She shrugs her soldiers and nods her head in ascent as the flame from her lighter is restored.

I went through the sordid details of my afternoon with Freddy again. I keep my eyes averted away from Momma, for once thankful for the darkness surrounding me. I'm shaking uncontrollably by the time I'm finished. I feel the warmth of my tears on my face, brushing them away I finally look over at her. She is ferociously putting out a cigarette on the cement stair. There is nothing left of it. The tobacco is scattered, and the cotton-like filter of the cigarette butt is flying around. Momma throws what is left onto the grass and turns to look at me. The light coming from the kitchen door to the porch caught the side of her face, and I could barely make out the scowl of her brow. I knew this has upset her, I just don't know who with, Freddy or me. We sat there in silence which seemed to last a lifetime. I knew she was picking her words carefully.

When she finally spoke, you could have knocked me over with a feather. "Audrey, your sure it was that picture? Did you see it? No one told you about it? No Audrey don't look at me like that. I believe you. It's just that I can't believe Freddy would do this."

"Well believe it, Momma, he did. Why can't you believe it? He's done and said some pretty awful things to us, girls. Who would tell me about the picture? Who else has he showed it to Momma!" I knew, but I wanted her to admit that he had shown it to Ceely, and she knew about it. Of course, she isn't going to admit to anything. She still looks at me as that little girl who was burned. I know Momma can't see past that and maybe that's a good thing for me.

"Uh, no one. I just meant maybe Freddy told you about it not showed it to you." Knowing I have seen this picture has shocked her. No, my momma wasn't expecting this. Ceely was right again.

"Momma do you want me to go into detail and describe the picture because I will if that's what you want? Do you want me to tell you what he was doing and where he was standing? Would that help you to believe me? Momma I have had some really bad things happen to me in my life, and this one is right at the top." She is upsetting me.

I never thought I would feel this way, but at this moment I want someone to take us away even if it means separating us. Just thinking that made me sick to my stomach. It's unfair, and I was getting very frustrated.

"No Audrey, you don't have to tell me any more. I will talk to Freddy. He will not do anything like this again. I know you don't understand men Audrey, but sometimes young girls don't realize how they dress or move can affect men. I'm not saying that that excuses what he did. It's just that I want you to be more careful in the things you wear around Freddy after all, this is a house full of women, and he's not used to that." She was patting me on my arm as if I just lost my best friend and not almost molested by a man.

No, not just any man her boyfriend. The monster she brought into this house full of 'women', her daughters. Momma stood up and said she is tired and is going to bed. She asked me to wash her blue pants and white blouse for tomorrow. Yuk! I hated washing clothes. We didn't have a washing machine, so we had to do them by hand in the bathtub. Then if they weren't dry by morning, we had to iron them dry, which took forever. Oh well, at least it will help me get rid of some of my frustration. I went inside and got Momma's clothes out of the dirty clothes hamper. Ran the water as hot as I could get it and started scrubbing.

I can hear Momma and Freddy's raised voices. Momma said to him, "Freddy never and I mean never go near Audrey again."

Freddy yells back at her, "Carly I was just trying to teach her a lesson, because she was teasing me. I told you already she was prancing around here in her tight short shorts. Just what do you expect me to do?

Momma's voice lowered like she is talking to one of us kids. "I expect you to behave like a man and control yourself. My God she's just a kid, Freddy."

Tight short shorts? Teasing him! What is he saying? I don't own a pair of tight anything. All my clothes are handed down to me from Donna. None of them fit right, besides I would never dress like that and Momma knows it. The next thing I hear made the blood in my veins turn cold. Freddy yells at Carmen to stay out of it. Oh my gosh, Carmen is in there with them. I didn't hear what she said, but she must have been taking up for me. I didn't hear her say anything else, though. The next thing I hear is the bedroom door slam, and Freddy's car start up. Good, maybe he's gone for *good I thought.* I knew that was naïve thinking on my part. He knew he had it good here. We've heard it enough from all our Uncles. That hurt the most. Instead of helping us, because they know what is going on. They made fun of us. They like to call us *Freddy's Harem.* They have to know how that makes us feel, but they don't care. No one did. I've become to dislike a few of my Uncles, a lot.

You know thinking things can't get much worse is a stupid thing to think around my house. That's like getting up in the morning and saying *oh what a beautiful day,* and inevitably it just goes downhill from there, so I have learned not to say or think either one.

Well a couple of months after my talk with Momma, or as she refers to it our first *Mother/ Daughter' talk,* Ceely tells Momma she's pregnant by her boyfriend. I didn't find out until a week later. Momma wants to keep it quiet. Get this she is ashamed of Ceely. Momma calls her a slut and wants Ceely to get an *abortion.* When Donna said she would never kill a baby Momma wants her to get married. Well, when that isn't going to happen either Momma comes up with the bright idea that we will move away, to Arizona no less. I can't believe it. *Why Arizona?* No one moves to Arizona. We don't even know anyone there. I guess that doesn't matter; Momma told us to pack and be ready to leave by the weekend. Daddy is mad. Grandmother just cried and cried. She tried to talk some sense into Momma, but we all know how well that goes. On a bright and sunny Saturday morning in my eighth-grade year, we are moving yet again, not just to another school district but this time to a whole new state. ARIZONA!

Chapter 13

"When you've lost your way; and there's nowhere to turn. You can't find a bridge; they've burned. In the end, you know this will be, another hard lesson you've been forced to learn."

It seems like it took forever to get to Arizona. Maybe that's because none of us wanted to go. We had to leave a lot behind this time, Daddy, Grandmother, Granddaddy, but worst of all our little brother Junior. Junior hated Freddy and I think Freddy hated him. Junior refused to go and Momma didn't make him. I think she didn't want to fight with Daddy. He was already mad because Freddy was going with us.

We also found out why Momma chose Arizona. Freddy wanted to live there, so once again Momma let him hurt us. I was afraid what Freddy might try to do to us in Arizona. He knew, without Daddy there, he could get away with anything. All the way to Arizona he tried to act like we were on some vacation and he was our tour guide. We were forever stopping to look at some stupid landmark or scenic view. I was miserable the whole way, but not as miserable as Ceely. We had to keep stopping so she could throw-up. That made Freddy mad. I didn't care though let him be mad. We also had Steven Allen with us. Steven was Aunt Jeans, baby boy. She had given him to Momma a year ago. I didn't know who his Daddy was, but Momma said he was by some man Aunt Reba was dating. She said she couldn't take care of him, and moved back to California. Tracy Earl became to be like a brother to us. I thought *Aunt Reba was crazy, how can you just give your baby away like that*, but I didn't think about it much. I just loved him a lot.

We stayed at a motel in Tempe, Arizona our first two days there until Momma rented us a house. Arizona is a beautiful State, but I didn't care I hated it. Everything about it was different from Texas, and it is hot. I started to school after we settled in. Carmen and Ceely didn't. They never went back to school after we moved to Arizona. Momma just let them quit.

My school was called Mc Clintock Junior High. It was a really beautiful school, brand new. Everything in Arizona looked brand new, though. I learned a lot from my teachers here, and we get to do all our gym classes outside. I like that too. I try to ignore what is going on at home, though. At first, Momma and Freddy seem happy, and he doesn't bother Ceely and me. Oh sure he treats us like we are his servants but he doesn't try anything dirty with me. He is mean to Ceely, though. Always treating her like she isn't anything and Momma lets him. I notice Momma take Ceely to only one doctor's appointment and then never again.

I asked Ceely why and she said, "They wanted my baby, Audie. That's why we came out here. When Momma took me to the doctor, she put down on the application that my name was Carly, and my last name was Freddy's. She listed Freddy as my husband. I guess she thought I would just go along with it, but when the doctor called me by Momma's name I told him that wasn't my name. Momma got mad when the doctor wanted to know what was going on. We left, and she never took me back. Now she tells everyone my husband is in the military that's why he isn't around."

"Ceely I'm sorry. You were smart to do that. Don't let her get away with anything, Ceely. I don't know what Aunt Reba was thinking giving her Steven Allen. Momma can't even raise us, and Freddy is weird." I knew then I had to help Ceely; she seemed sad. I also knew, she would fight like a Momma tiger for her baby. She proven that.

Two months after moving here I find out why Carmen was in the bedroom with Freddy all those times. I had just come in from school and was changing clothes. Ceely came into the bedroom and threw herself down on the bed. She started crying. I ran over to her and asked what's wrong?

She raised her head and said, "Go ask Momma and Freddy. They're the ones that are happy about it. How could Carmen do this, Audie? It just turns my stomach, but I knew it was going to happen sooner or later."

I was staring at her wondering if she knows I don't have a clue about what she is saying. I turn and go into the living room where Momma, Carmen, and Freddy are. Freddy is smiling and Talking to Carmen. She is sitting on his lap. Momma is sitting in a chair across from them, and she doesn't look so happy to me.

"Momma? Ceely is upset about something that's wrong?" I was trying not to sound nervous

She looks over at Carmen and says you tell her. Carmen stops smiling and won't look at me. I'm getting upset. "Will someone tell me what's going on?"

Oh, Freddy had no problem blurting out his so-called good news, "We're going to have a baby." I looked at Momma. I know I had disgust written all over my face when Freddy says, "No, not your Momma. Carmen and me!"

I can't move or think straight. The words began pouring out of my mouth like a water faucet, "How could you? Carmen is just a kid. You're too old for her, and y'all aren't married. Momma, this can't be true. Tell them they can't have a baby. There has to be a law or something. Oh, I'm gonna be sick!" I didn't even know what I was saying. I didn't even care if I hurt Carmen. It is all so sick. Why didn't Carmen tell Freddy no like Ceely and I did? It can't Be happening. Freddy's thirty years older than Carmen. He's ten years older than Momma and Daddy!

That's when I run into the bathroom and get sick. I don't know what to think. All I can see is Freddy's grin. He is enjoying what this is doing to me, to all of us. Oh Carmen, how could you let him touch you? I open the bathroom door to leave, and Carmen is standing there. She looks mad. I hadn't seen this Carmen in a long time.

"Sis, I love him, and we are going to get married! Whether or not, you and Ceely like it" That's all she says and then turns and walks to the bedroom.

I stand frozen in place for a moment and then walk into the kitchen. Feeling lost, I aimlessly wander out the back door. Letting it slam behind me. Everything seems dirty. It all makes sense now, though. *Oh my, God*, this has been going on for a long time. Ceely's pregnancy isn't why we moved here. It's because Freddy is sleeping with Carmen. He and Momma could have got in a lot of trouble. I should have known it was something like this. Momma used Ceely's pregnancy that's all. Why doesn't any of this surprise me, because I knew? I just didn't want to admit it. Ceely is right there is some sick stuff going on in our house, and I chose not to see it. Well isn't that how Momma raised us. To keep our mouths shut about what went on in our house. I guess I did better than that; I pretended nothing was happening. Oh God, where do we go from here?

Things went on as usual. Like nothing was different except both my sisters are having babies. I throw myself into being happy about Ceely's baby. I tell her I feel she is going to have a girl. She says if I am right she will name her after me. I was amazed at Ceely's stomach it just got bigger and bigger. The day I got to feel the baby move is exciting. It made it all real. In April Ceely gave birth to a *beautiful baby girl*, and true to her word she names her after me. Her name is *Victoria Rose*. She is gorgeous. Perfect in every way. She looks just like her Momma.

Ceely had wanted to name Victoria Rose after Steven Allen also. She didn't though because we lost him and it hurt too much. My great Aunt Abby, Aunt Reba's Mother, came to Arizona and took him away from us. It broke our hearts. We begged Momma not to let him go, but to protect Freddy we lost Steven. Apparently, Freddy is an ex-convict, and he isn't supposed to be in Arizona. Aunt Abby threatened to go to the police if Momma didn't turn Steven over to he,r so of course Momma did. My Great Aunt Abby didn't know Aunt Reba had given Steven to Momma right after she gave birth to him in Dallas. She thought Aunt Reba took him to California with her. Well, I guess Aunt Reba came back to Dallas and told Aunt Abby where Steven was. I don't blame my Great Aunt Abby I wouldn't want my grandchild living with us either, but it still broke my heart. I know Great Aunt Abby threatened to turn my Momma into authorities one time because of Freddy and Grandmother told her sister she better not have us taken away. Great Aunt Abby is my Grandmother's older sister. Atleast I have my niece. I love having her to hold when life gets to tough. It feels good to be an Aunt.

Our school had been out for a couple of weeks when Grandmother shows up in Arizona. I was shocked! She says she flew out here to get Cossette and me. I don't know what surprises me most that Momma is going to let us go or that Grandmother flew on an airplane. She's deathly afraid of flying. I want to go, but I don't want to leave Ceely and Victoria Rose. Momma said they would be coming home after Carmen has her baby. Grandmother isn't happy about that either. I hear her and Momma arguing, and Grandmother never argues with Momma unless it is about us kids. I think that's why Momma is letting her take Cossette and me. Grandmother threatened her with Carmen's pregnancy by Freddy. I have never heard Grandmother raise her voice with my Momma like this. It makes me feel good that someone is finally standing up to Momma. My Grandmother asks her how she is going to explain this to Cameron. Momma says it is none of his business. My Grandmother says oh yes it is, after all, he is Carmen's Daddy. Momma told her he hadn't been a Daddy to these kids for years. Grandmother was furious with Momma, but she let it drop. She knew it wouldn't do any good to argue, and she didn't speak to Freddy the two days she was here.

Ceely cried when I left, and so did I. We both knew she would be home soon, but the thought of Ceely being there alone is a nightmare. I hated leaving my little brother Craig too. I felt like I would never see them again.

One thing I know for sure I don't want ever to come back to Arizona again, as long as I live. I think I cried the whole trip home, but once I got to Grandmothers house, I felt safe again. My life felt clean. The first thing I did was go out to my Granddaddy's flower garden. I ran through it until I was out of breath. Nothing could touch me here. No one could hurt me. I lay down in Granddaddy's thick, lush grass and watched the clouds in the sky. I was home, for a while hopefully.

Chapter 14

"Your memory can be your enemy. It's as sly as a fox. Those memories you've kept hidden can rise from the dark, and all that you hold beautifully will lose its spark."

I had waited six long months to see my family. Then out of the blue Momma shows up today from Arizona. She hadn't called anyone. The whole family drove up to Grandmothers as if they had never left. Granddaddy was trying to question Momma on why she didn't let them know she was coming. I didn't care why. I am just glad to see them. Running out to the car and seeing Ceely holding Victoria Rose was as if we have never been apart. Victoria Rose might be older, but she's still tiny. She is adorable, and I love her so much.

After staying with our Grandparents a few days Momma found a house, four blocks from them. Thankfully I won't have to change schools. When Momma left Arizona, she left a lot of my stuff there, important stuff. Like my *birth certificate* and my *diploma from seventh grade*. These things meant a lot to me, but very little to her apparently. She said it was an accident. My papers were in a small filing cabinet that got left behind. She said she would try and get them replaced for me. I got a copy of my birth certificate. The diploma won't be able to be replaced.

I turned fifteen a couple of months ago, and it seems to have changed things for me. I feel everyone treats me different, sort of like an adult now. Ceely is floating on a cloud these days; she's dating Levi again. Ceely and I work at Kentucky Fried Chicken. Ceely got the job first and then got me on as soon as I had my birthday. We both had to lie about our age, though. I told them I was sixteen. I didn't want to lie, but sometimes you have too. One-night Ceely and I both were working, and Levi came in. He asked Ceely if he could pick her up after work so that they could talk. I guess a friend told him she was working there. After that night they were inseparable. Levi fell in love with Victoria Rose. Of course, he did, who wouldn't. Getting back with Levi didn't change things at home for her. Momma was still hard on Ceely.

Last month they got into a big argument, so Ceely took Victoria Rose and left. They stayed with Levi's mother until Ceely could afford an apartment for them. I miss them a lot, but at least I have somewhere else to go now. Ceely rented their new place in Mesquite. When you don't have a drivers license or a car that is a long way from Oak Cliff. Momma let me stay with Ceely on the weekends. Daddy usually drives me out there. Ceely has gotten a job with Safeway Grocery Store as a cashier. I still work at Kentucky Fried Chicken, and my paycheck still goes to my Momma.

Freddy married Carmen right after they returned from Arizona. No one was happy but them, I was mortified. The only bright spot is they have a little boy now. His name is *Charles Allen*. Like our cousin *Steven Allen,* he also is named after *Freddy. Allen* is *Freddy's* middle name.

Right after Charles was born Carmen was pregnant again. She went into labor this morning, and Mom and Freddy took her to the hospital. I've been excited waiting for Mom to call and let us know if the baby has arrived yet. Mom finally calls but the news isn't good. She said during the delivery the baby died. The doctor told them that the umbilical cord got wrapped around the babies neck. All I heard was Carmen's baby girl has died. I don't know how to handle this. Mom says they named her *Serena,* and they should be home soon.

"Mom, how is Carmen?" She didn't respond; I thought she had hung up. "Mom? Are you there?"

"Yes Audie, I'm here. Carmen will be fine. How is everything there? Are the kids giving you any trouble? Mom's voice is breaking.

I could tell she didn't want to say any more about Carmen or the baby. "Mom everything's fine here. Tell Carmen; I love her."

I put the receiver in the cradle. I drop to my knee's and close my eye's to stop the tears. I ask God, *why? Why do these bad things have to happen to us? Oh, dear God why did you have to take this baby? My sister has wanted a little girl for so long! Dear Lord, she would have been the best Momma to her. Why? Oh, why?* I feel His presence. I know this is for the best. Wiping my eye's, I walk to the back door to check on the kids. Watching them play, I think how lucky Mom is to have us. *Life is too short; anybody can die at any moment.* Hearing the front door open brought my thoughts back to Carmen. Turning around slowly I look into the living room. My eyes connect with Freddy's.

Swallowing my contempt for him I choke out, "I'm sorry for your loss Freddy. Is my sister okay? Why are you home already?"

Freddy tries to hug me, but I push him away as he says, "C'mon Audie, I need to be comforted. Carmen will be fine. It'll take her time, but she will work through it. Your Mom is with her. I'm going back later."

Squeezing past him I say, "The kids are out back playing. I haven't said anything to them; I thought you or Mom should."

Almost running to my bedroom, I slam the door and throw myself across the bed. The tears came; I couldn't stop. Sorrowful tears fell freely. They made my whole body shake out of control. Rolling my body up into a ball, they slid down my face onto my pillow, drenching it within seconds. No sound came from me, though. I wasn't going to let Freddy hear me cry. I wasn't going to give him a reason to come to my bedroom. I don't need him. *I want my Momma!* With that thought in my head, I sleep.

I pretty much have thrown myself into working and going to school. When

Carmen came home from the hospital a few weeks ago, she just ghosted around the house. She and I didn't talk about her losing Selena. I just didn't know what to say, and she looks so sad all the time. Instead, I try to take some of the burdens off by helping her around the house. Boy, my diary sure has gotten a lot of use lately. Not just writing in it, but I have gone back and read it a lot too. It has made me realize how much I've learned from my sister's choices.

When Ceely lived with us, I took care of Victoria Rose while she worked or went out on dates. I saw how hard it was for her to juggle work, raising a child, and still trying to do things for herself at such a young age. I'm not sure what I wanted to do with my future, but because of the bad choices my Mother made and eventually caused her older daughters to make, I know I don't want ever to, have to walk down the path they have. Not that I would ever think that my nieces or nephews were bad choices or mistakes, I love them very much. I am talking about the dark situations my Mother put my sisters in; for them to feel this was the only road they could take. I know our lives would have been different if Mother hadn't brought this man, Freddy, into our home.

What most baffles me is *Carmen truly loves Freddy.* It still confuses me *how* or *why* but she does. All I know he is the luckiest man in the world, because he doesn't deserve her love or the children she gave him. My only savior is God. I know He is watching over me, and He has a plan. I just wish he would reveal it soon. I watch my older sister and want to cry. She looks so lonely; even though the house is full of people. She's has become quiet.

Carmen does pretty much all the cooking and cleaning. I help when I can, but the majority falls on her. Mom and Freddy treat her as if she's their personal slave. I know Carmen feels differently, but that's what I see. The only time I notice Carmen happy and carefree is when she's with her son. It doesn't matter what she's doing with him, feeding, bathing, or just playing, he is her life. I think it's sad because Brenda is a beautiful person inside and out. Freddy doesn't deserve my sister, and she deserves so much more. I will never tell her this because she would not understand how I feel. I can't bring myself to hurt her and tell her what a monster she has chosen to spend the rest of her life loving. I don't know why she doesn't see him for what he is. I guess she has chosen to accept her fate, and to make the best life she can for her son. Her son will always come first in her life, even above Momma and Freddy. If anyone tries to hurt him, she will fight like a Momma lion to protect him.

I'm still confused about Mother and Freddy's relationship. Is he Son-In-Law or do Mom and Freddy have a relationship? I don't know and at this point, I don't care. The latter would just be too sick for me to think about, even though the signs are there.

We're moving back to Pleasant Grove this weekend, where we lived before Arizona. I'm happy because its closer to Ceely and Victoria Rose, but I will have to change schools again, and in High School, this is a major problem. I can barely keep up as it is, but when you stay at a school for a couple of months and then move again, it's all most impossible to get a good education. The worst part is I will have to quit my job. That job was my salvation it helped me tolerate being at home. Momma says I will get another one, but it's not that easy for a fifteen-year-old.

I enroll in Spruce High School on Monday. Today is Friday, and I'm going to spend the weekend with my Daddy. Thank goodness I won't have to help them move again, only because Momma wants me to watch Cossette and Craig at Daddy's this weekend. He lives with Maw Maw. I don't mind, though, I worry when they stay over there. I don't trust my Uncle Herman or Daddy around them. I'm not sure, but I don't think Maw Maw does either. Anytime I stay with her she makes me sleep in her room. She's never given me an explanation for this, but she doesn't have too. It's just another one of those unspoken rules. She knows what's going on, and she will help silently, but don't ask for more than that. Believe me, if nothing else I have learned with parents like mine, you don't question them, and you sure don't open your mouth to anyone else. Junior still lives with Daddy. I guess he always will. I wish Momma would talk to Junior. He thinks she doesn't love him; that she picked Freddy over him. He can't understand why I live at home with Momma and Freddy, but I have nowhere to go. Nowhere. He doesn't understand why I won't live with Daddy and him. He says Daddy isn't as he was before. He doesn't hit him much anymore, only when he needs it. I guess he never will understand why I can't live with our Daddy. I will never tell him how Daddy treated me. Maybe I could have lived with them if Daddy had just hit me. No, I will never tell Junior the horrible things Daddy put me through. He's too young, and he worships our Daddy. I won't take that from him.

In his eye's Momma is the bad guy, not Daddy. Junior confided in me that he feels it's our Momma who drove Daddy crazy so that she could be with Freddy. I've tried to explain Daddy's sickness to him, but my little brother has his mind made up to put all the blame on Mom. No matter what I say. Hopefully some day he will understand. I've noticed guys react to a situation so much differently than a girl. It's like someone has to be blamed for anything bad that happens to them and then they have to take it out on the world or the closest person to them. Guys don't stop to think that maybe no one is to blame when things go wrong. Stuff happens that we have no control of, sometimes it scares me why I know or feel these things. Aunt Reba used to tell my Mom I knew too much for a kid my age, whenever I would voice my opinion. Daddy says it's a gift I have, and I should not question it. I do question it because it scares me to know things I shouldn't be able to understand, giving my head a shake brings me back to where I am.

What a beautiful day. I decided to come out to the back yard to write in my diary while I wait for Daddy to arrive. There's a cool breeze for once. It's September and the days have been so hot and muggy. I'm going to miss this house. I love all the trees around it. We are in an old neighborhood, so there are trees and honeysuckle vines everywhere. All the yards here are so green and lush. Sometimes even now I pretend I'm a butterfly, and I fly from every sweet honeysuckle and taste its nectar. When I have had my fill of the nectar, I turn back into a girl again. Not just any girl, but I'm beautiful, and I wear very pretty dresses like those models on TV and everyone wants to be my friend. When I talk, they all hang onto every word I say. It's like I'm very important and loved by all, but like I said it's just a dream. My dreams are to finish High School and go to college. I would love to write books. Reading is so important to me because it takes me to places I know I will never see. To be able to learn about other people and how they live is so interesting. I know what my reality is, though. I just hope I get to finish High School and become an *Airline Stewardess,* or maybe a *Secretary.* One thing I do know is I will have to make a better life for myself. No one will or can do this but me. It's my choice. It is the only choice I will accept.

My Momma says I'm a dreamer; maybe that's true, but it's my dreams that keep me sane. She thinks women were put here to serve men or should I say her daughters were. Momma never served anyone. I love my Momma. I hate what she accepts as normal and what she expects from me.

I Lay down across the green grass and close my eyes. I can feel the light from the sun pushing through my lids. The coolness of the freshly mowed grass is filtering through my clothes. I love the smell of cut grass. It smells so fresh and clean, like the earth after a light rain. I feel so in touch with Mother Nature at this moment. This feeling must be what it feels like to be in Heaven. These moments are rare for me. Usually, there's noise everywhere. Not that we are loud kids, but when you have six kids in one house someone is always talking.

I let out a sigh hearing my little brother Craig squeal with delight. Daddy must be here. Well, better come back to earth before Mommas' accusations of daydreaming become a reality I have to admit I have. Suddenly the light that was trying to penetrate my eyelids has gone dark. Rising up on one elbow and squinting I try to see what had blocked the sun. I brought my other hand up to my forehead to shelter my eyes and get a better look. I feel like a sea captain looking for land. It's Daddy standing over me. A feeling of panic runs through me, so I start scooting backward, like one of those crabs I've seen in a book on sea creatures.

Grabbing me by one of my ankles Daddy says half laughing, "Whoa girl, where do you think you're scrambling to? Here take my hand and I will help you up."

I'm trying hard not to show him how shaken I am by his presence. I didn't understand it myself. "Oh, Daddy! You just scared me. I didn't hear the back door shut. I'm ready to go. Just give me a minute, okay?" I jump up so fast I almost knock him down.

I run up the back stairs and into the house. I don't stop until I get to my bedroom. Once the door is closed, I just slide to the floor and sit there, trying to stop my body from shaking. *What is wrong with me? It is a just Daddy. He caught me off guard.* That's all it is I tell myself, standing up I grab my bag and leave. On the drive over I don't have to speak, thankfully. Daddy and Craig talk about the tree house Daddy has built for us kids in Maw Maw's backyard. Cossette keeps rolling her eyes. She doesn't want to be here. She wants to stay with our cousin LaDonna at Uncle Adam's house, but Momma said no. She wants us all together. I don't understand it either, but I'm sure not going to argue with Momma like Cossette does. It gets you nowhere in the end. Pulling up in front of Maw Maw's house I think, *this is different it's nice.* The house is old but comfortable looking. Maw Maw moves around like we do. Daddy leads us to a bedroom in the back of the house that looks like a screened in porch. I can see tall oak trees in the back yard. Looking up, I can see the clouds, floating in the sky like small white puffs of cotton. Wow, this will be like sleeping outside.

Daddy thumped me on my head and said, "You like the room, Audie? It's my room, and we all will be sleeping here tonight."

Looking at Daddy and then to the bed I say, "Yeah, I think this is neat, butt Daddy there's only one bed. We won't all fit." I shift nervously from foot to foot.

Daddy laughs, "Don't worry Audrey you won't have to sleep with the boys. I am just joking with you. The boy's and I will sleep here Your Maw Maw is going to her sisters tonight. You and Cossette will be sleeping in her room."

"But Daddy, I want to sleep out here. Can't Y'all sleep in Maw Maw's room?"

All of a sudden Maw Maw's scratchy voice fills the room, "No, that won't do. You girls get your things and come with me. Cameron tell those boys to get their filthy shoes off my bed. That's all I need, more mouths to feed." Maw Maw grumbled all the way to her room.

Cossette looks at me and says, "Oh great I feel welcome. What? Does she think I want to be here?" She looks at Maw Maws back and sticks out her tongue. I tell Cossette to be quiet.

She says, "Why? She can't hear me. She's going deaf remember."

Before I can tell Cossette Maw Maw has selective hearing Maw Maw whips around and gives Cossette the nastiest look and says, "That's why I told your Daddy I don't want you here. No respect, you give me no respect. I should rinse your mouth out with soap. Like I did your Daddy when he was little. I will not put up with that smart mouth of yours Cossette." Without taking a breath she continues, "No matter what my son says, I will not! But of course, the only time your Daddy has a backbone is when it comes to you kids. It's my house, and if you don't respect it, I will kick you out of it."

Maw Maw had turned back around when Cossette says, "Please kick me out. I don't want to be here anyway."

I give Cossette a kick and say, "Shhhh, don't make this any worse than it already is. Daddy's happy that we are here. At least try to act as you are too."

Apparently, Maw Maw didn't hear Cossette this time because she just continued berating our presence here and how her sons take advantage of her. Maw Maw's room is huge. It has two doors, one that leads to the front porch and the other one goes out into the hallway. She is telling us not to mess with any of her things and to be sure and lock both doors before we go to bed. Her demands went on and on. I almost missed what she was saying when she turns the lecture directly to me. Cossette pokes me in the ribs and nods toward Maw Maw.

"Audrey, you're the oldest, so I'm counting on you to make sure my rules are followed. Above all, I want you to make sure the hallway door is always shut tight and when your sleeping it is locked. Are you listening, Audrey? I want you to repeat what I just said."

I take a deep breath and say, "I will make sure the hallway door is shut, and it is locked when we go to bed."

Cossette looks at her. I know by the look on her face she is fixing to irritate Maw Maw. "Why is it so important that we lock the hallway door?" Here we go.

Maw Maw spins around, all Five feet of her, and stomps over to Cossette. I think she startles her. Cossette wasn't expecting that.

Maw Maw got right in front of her and simply says, "Because I said to!"

Then she turns to me. "Audrey, your Uncle's cat, tries to get in here at night. I don't want him to shed that nasty hair all over my bed."

"Okay, Maw Maw I will try to keep him out. Maw Maw if you don't mind I think I will tell Daddy to sleep in here. We would like to sleep in with the boys. I like that room." I do. I think it will be neat sleeping under the stars.

With her hand on her hips she chokes out her command, "Absolutely not, you will do as I say! It's for you're on good. If my sister weren't sick, I would stay home, but I can't she needs me. Just do what I say." The latter part was said as if to herself.

Cossette and I walk back to Daddy's bedroom. "Don't worry Audie; we'll ask Daddy. He will let us sleep back here; besides Maw Maw's room stinks like old people's medicine. We can't sleep in there. Daddy will let us. He lets us do whatever we want. You know that."

Yeah, I did know that. That's the problem; Daddy's too lenient at times. Daddy is like a big kid. Whenever someone says no to us, he will say yes. I know he will let us, but I don't want Maw Maw to be mad at me. I know she is doing this for us out of worry, and again I don't know why. Battling between doing what is right or sleeping in Daddy's room is giving me a headache. Oh darn, Maw Maw will kill me.

"Okay we will ask him, but we have to get up before she gets home, so Maw Maw want know. I still hesitate, something is telling me to sleep in Maw Maw's room, but I just shrugged it away.

"Audie, you are such a chicken. What does it matter what she thinks? But if you want we will get up early." I'm not a chicken. I guess I have more respect for her wishes than Cossette does.

Of course, Daddy says yes. He put Craig in with him. Junior, Cossette and I get to sleep in the back room. I sleep on the outside, and Junior sleeps in the middle. Cossette is way over next to the screened window. She still has accidents in the bed, so neither one of us wanted to sleep to close to her. I feel bad for her, but I don't want to get wet either. Junior and Craig makes fun of her and calls her names. We all lay in bed and talk for a while. Junior still wants me to come live with him and Daddy. I tell him I can't. Momma needs me home to help Carmen. Cossette says she wouldn't live with Maw Maw if you paid her, but she would like to live with Daddy instead of Momma and Freddy. I tell them there's no need even to talk about it because Momma will never let it happen.

I feel bad for Junior when he says, "Well Audrey, she let me."

"Junior you know that's different. Believe me; she wouldn't have if she needed you for something. Not that she doesn't love you because she does. I think that's why she let you go because she does love you. Junior you know you two boys mean a lot to Momma, rather you realize that are not. Someday when Craig gets older and asks to live with Daddy, she will let him go too."

"Audie, you live in a dream world. She doesn't love me and it won't happen. Craig will always be her favorite!" He turned over on his side.

"Okay, I see I'm doing nothing but upsetting you so let's just go to sleep." Cossette is already fast asleep. I lay there until I hear juniors easy breathing and know he is asleep, also.

I don't know how long I had been asleep, but something woke me. I'm being pulled to the end of the bed. I feel someone reach up and slowly pull my underwear down toward my ankles. I'm trying to wake up. Maybe I'm dreaming, but then I realize this is for real it is happening to me, again. I push my foot forward to scoot back up on the bed. I pretend I'm waking up. I tell Junior to quit pulling the covers off me. That didn't work.

Whoever was at the foot of the bed is pulling me back down. I can feel his breath on my inner thighs. I keep thinking, oh my God what do I do?

Finally, I kick out and try to say with my sternest voice without waking up Junior and Cossette. "Daddy stop it, leave me alone. Daddy, I can get pregnant now. If you touch me again, you will be in big trouble." I don't know why I think it's Daddy. I just feel it is.

No! I'm not going to let this happen to me again. Not this time! Not ever again! He will not get away with hurting me. I don't know where I get the strength or the courage, but I kick out as hard as I can. I hear him fall backward. I can't see anything. I realize there must not be a moon out tonight. It's funny the things that go through your mind at a time of crises. It was all happening so fast, but I feel like I'm crawling. It feels like one of those dreams where you are trying to run but getting nowhere. I jump out of bed, stopping to grab my underwear, as they slide down my left leg. I run as fast and quietly as I can to Maw Maw's room. I can barely make out a faint shaft of light coming from the kitchen. As I turn to run into her bedroom, my whole body is knocked backward by the closed door. Bouncing right back up, not feeling a thing, I turn the knob, run inside, close and lock the door behind me. Quietly, trying not to make a sound I back away from the door. Hearing footsteps coming down the hall toward me I climb upon the bed. Something soft moves and then lets out a howl. *Darn, it's the cat!* Grabbing it, I run to the door that opens to the front porch and throws the *cat* out. The footsteps stop at the bedroom door.

"Audrey what's wrong with you. Open the door it's Dad." Oh my, God, it was Daddy, and he's talking like nothing happened.

"Daddy go away, leave me alone. I'm scared. You scared me; please just go away. I'm going to sleep with Craig tonight." I'm shaking. I hear Daddy walk off.

Thank goodness, it sounds like he is walking toward the living room. *Oh please, don't let him go back to his room. Cossette is still back there.* Looking around, I try to find something I can protect myself with if I have to. I know Maw Maw used to keep a bat under her bed. All I know is I'm not leaving this bedroom without protection, and the only thing that will pull me out of here is if I think he's going to hurt Cossette. I will wake up the whole neighborhood if I have to. I hear Daddy walk across the living room to the front door. I turn around and look at the other door leading to the front porch. It's slightly open.

Oh my, God, it's open! I could have sworn I shut and locked that when I threw the *cat* out. Feeling like I'm running in slow motion, again. I slide and fall just as I get to the door. Kicking it shut with my foot; I jump up and lock it as Daddy comes onto the porch from the living room. The door has a small window in it. Maw Maw has a sheer curtain over it. I can just make out Daddy's shadow. He lit a cigarette. I stand there as if frozen watching the red tip of it burn.

I jump when Daddy speaks, "Audrey Rose, open this door. I'm not going to hurt you. I just need to talk to you. I will stand out here the rest of the night if I have to. I said to open this door! Now!"

What do I do? Tears start flowing down my face. Terrified, I sink to my knees, praying I ask God to help me. I stand up and keep thinking; someone will save me. *They have to I can't do this alone. I can't live through this again. Where is Uncle Herman? Can't he hear Daddy yelling and banging on the doors?* Daddy's shaking the doorknob brings me back to reality. I walk over to the bed bend down and search for Maw Maw's bat, and there it is. It feels cold in my hand. I let go of it and roll it back under the bed. Slowly I stand up, and my heart stops. I see a form sitting up in the bed. I thought I was going to die right there on the spot. Then my brain registered who it is. Craig, I forgot he was in here sleeping with Daddy. Scrambling up onto the bed and I grab him.

Hearing him let a whimper I try to comfort him. "Shhh, go back to sleep it's alright. No don't get up, just lay back down. There that's better. Sister is here with you, okay?"

We just quietly hold each other for a minute. "Audie, will you stay with me tonight. Where's Daddy? Is he mad at you"?

Pulling him to me, I gently say, "Yes, I will stay here next to you. Daddy is outside having a cigarette. No, Daddy's not mad. He just doesn't feel good, and you know when he is like this Momma says to stay away from him. It will be all right, close your eyes. There that's better." Craig's body relaxed. He is asleep.

Quietly slipping out of bed I walk to the door with the window. Just as I peek out, I hear the other doors knob rattle, as if someone is trying to open it.

With my heart dropping to my stomach calmly say, "Daddy go to bed. You are scaring Craig. I will stay with him tonight. Daddy if you don't I am going to call Momma to get us. Is that what you want?"

"Audie, I don't know what you're saying. I'm just making sure you locked the door like your Maw Maw said to do. I am going to sleep right here on the couch. If you need me just call out, and I will come running. I thought I heard something earlier. I'm going to check on Cossette and Junior first."

"No! No Daddy, that was me you heard I was checking on them. Just go ahead and go to bed they are fine." *I don't know where I was getting the things I was saying or the control I had in my voice. I just knew I had to talk fast to keep him from Cossette.*

He says goodnight and walks into the living room. I heard the couch squeak and knew he has laid down on it. Then I hear the click of a lighter, as he lit another cigarette. I fought sleep. I know I had to stay awake. Everything was going through my head. I'm so afraid he will go back and hurt Cossette. I strain my ears to hear every time he moves in his sleep. I know he has gone to sleep when I hear him snoring. *Finally, I think, after what seems like a pack of cigarettes later.*

I sat all night on the floor with my back to the hallway door, so I was facing the porch door. I only move twice. Once is to check on Craig when he moans in his sleep. I didn't want him to cry and wake up Daddy. The second time I move is to stretch. All I know is at the break of dawn I'm calling Momma to get us. I must have drifted off because the next thing I hear is Cossette banging on the door to let her in.

"Audie, open the door. Why didn't you wake me up? Hurry I hear Uncle Herman talking to Maw Maw and she is on her way home!" I stand up moaning. Every bone in my body hurt. *Is this what it feels like to be old*? I open the door, and Cossette almost falls into me. For someone who can care less what Maw Maw thinks she sure looks worried.

"Hey slow down. It's not like Maw Maw can fly over here. Where's Daddy?" She is standing there looking at me as if I had gone crazy.

"What do you mean, where's Daddy? He's asleep on the couch silly. What are you doing in here? I know you went to bed with Junior and me." Cossette is looking confused now and irritated.

"I know, but Craig woke up in the middle of the night, so Daddy wanted me to come lay with him. I guess I fell asleep." How easily that rolled off my tongue. Oh, how I hate lying.

"I guess the door locked itself. Oh never mind, let's just get Craig up and put him in bed with Junior. Then we can see if Maw Maw has any cereal. I'm hungry." That's my little sister. She knows her priorities.

After we get us a bowl of cereal we take it outside and climb into the tree house Daddy has built. We haven't been there long when Maw Maw is calling for us to come inside.

"What are you girls thinking? Get in here and make up my bed. Then you can clean those bowls you just used." Maw Maw is home.

"Audrey, you go wake up your Daddy first. Tell him I need him to go to the store for me. Now girl! Don't just stand there." I couldn't move for a minute.

When Maw Maw walks into the kitchen, I tell Cossette to tell Daddy what Maw Maw said. She says she will if she doesn't have to help with the bed. I tell her it's a deal; while I'm making her bed Maw Maw walks into the room.

She didn't ask why Cossette is doing what she told me to do. She just asks, "How did it go last night Audrey. Did y'all sleep all right in here? Did anyone bother you? I mean did the cat try to get in.?"

"No Maw Maw I slept- I mean we slept fine, and the cat didn't bother us. Maw Maw, will you tell me the story again about your mother coming to Texas in a covered wagon and how the Indians attacked them?"

I didn't want to have to lie again, and Maw Maw loves talking about her mother. Who by the way is still alive and is almost 100 years old. My Great Grandma is the cutest thing. She has white hair that hangs to her feet, which she always keeps in a bun, and she loves singing Sweet Sixteen to us. She is so different than her daughter, but maybe Maw Maw has had a hard life. I know six boys couldn't have been easy to raise. After hearing about how the Indians tried to kill them and take the women and children, my Great Grandma was just a baby at the time; I asked Maw Maw if I could call Momma. She says I can.

Momma says Daddy is supposed to bring us home, but I tell her I would rather she come and get us. She asked me if anything is wrong. I tell her I just want her to get us now. Besides, Daddy can't bring us home until later, and I need to get stuff ready for school, which isn't a lie. She says she is on her way. When Daddy gets back from the store, I tell him Momma is coming to get us. He isn't happy about it, but he understood I have to go to school tomorrow. Nothing was mentioned about the night before. He didn't even flinch when he talked to me for the first time that day, and I guess he didn't see me flinch either when he went to kiss me on the cheek to say goodbye.

Chapter 15

"You're afraid to be happy. You know it wants last.
He says he loves you. It's happening so fast.
You try to pull away. He takes you by the hand.
He says to trust him. You know love at last."

Today is the day. Ceely and Levi are getting married. I'm so happy for them, although Momma has tried to ruin it for Ceely. She called all my Daddy's family and told them that Ceely says *Daddy will not be walking her down the aisle because she is afraid he might embarrass her.* Worse yet, she said Ceely is not allowing Daddy to come to the wedding at all. Momma told them that none of Ceely's family would be there; not even her Grandparents, out of respect for our Daddy.

I immediately call Grandmother; as soon as she answers I start crying, "Grandma, what's going on? Have you talked to Momma about Ceely's wedding? She says I can't go, and neither are y'all."

"Yes honey, your Mother has called. Don't worry, your Granddaddy and I are going. I've also talked to your sister. It's just a big misunderstanding between them. You need to call Ceely and talk to her. She is very upset about all this. I'm sure we can straighten it out after the wedding."

With a heavy sigh she continues, "I'm upset with your Momma for letting this happen on her daughter's wedding day, but these things do happen. Not only will your Grandfather and I be there, but also Ceely has asked him to give her away. You should know baby; we will always be here for you kids. Nothing will keep us away from that church today."

Between anxious gulps of tears, I plead with her, "Grandma, I want to go too, but Mommas says I absolutely, cannot go. What do you mean Granddaddy is giving Ceely away? That means what Momma's saying is true! Oh, Grandma, Ceely can't feel that way about Daddy!" Feeling hurt and angry, I pull the phone from my ear to hang it up.

Then I hear Grandma's voice raised in anger through the ear of the phone. "Audrey Rose, you listen to me young lady, enough of this pointing fingers. Your sister needs you right now. This is her big day, don't you dare think of anyone but her. Now, baby, there has been a lot of hurtful things said and until we can all calm down and get to the bottom of it call your sister and I will talk to you Momma about you going, okay?" I have never heard my Grandmother use this tone with me before.

"Yes, you're right. I will call Ceely right now. Grandma, I'm sorry I yelled at you. Please, get Momma to let me go." With a feeling of shame, I gently hold the disconnect button down on the phone.

Taking a deep breath, I release it and dial Ceely's number. Hearing Ceely's voice on the other end of the phone starts me crying again. Grandmother is right none of this makes sense. Ceely says Daddy is still at Terrell State Hospital, and there is no way he can come to the wedding, or give her away. Ceely can't understand why Mother is saying these things about her. Hanging up the phone with Ceely I am sure of only, one thing *I will go to her wedding!* Sitting on the bed in my room, I drop my head and let the tears flow. My head is spinning with not knowing what's truth and what's a lie. *What do I believe? Who do I believe?* One fact stands out more than others, and that is *I will never take anything that is told to me as Gospel!* If I chose to believe Momma, then that would make Ceely a mean and unforgiving person.

Ceely had said some pretty mean things about Momma since she moved away, but I don't think she would hurt Daddy intentionally just to get back at Momma. If this is true how can I possibly go to her wedding? Although if I believe Ceely this would truly make Momma a monster, to want to ruin her daughter's *Wedding Day*. Well, until Daddy gets out of the hospital and I can talk to him I will believe Ceely. My sister has been here for me all my life and I will move *Heaven and Earth* to respect that. *Somehow, someway I will be at her wedding!*

Drying my eye's, I feel determined. Tiptoeing, I try to touch the ceiling with my fingertips. Releasing the tension in my body, I let myself collapse to the floor as if I were a *rag doll*. Lying there holding my breath for a few seconds I exhale slowly. Then slowly unroll my body until I'm standing again. Shaking all negative thoughts out of my head, I focus on how I can get Momma to change her mind. I know she doesn't care how I feel about the whole situation, and right now I don't care what she thinks, either. I can sneak out and walk to Grandmothers. No, Momma would kill me when I got back. Sneaking out will just make things worse. No, I guess I will just have to face Momma, and tell her I'm going no matter how she feels. I hate confrontation, and I know Momma will make me feel awful. Oh gosh, my stomach is in knots just thinking about having to make a stand with Momma. Walking over to the window on shaking legs I take a deep breath to calm my nerves, and then there's the disrespect thing toward Momma. How do Ceely and Cossette stand up to Momma and make it look so easy? *Oh why, do I have to be so weak?*

I sit back down feeling helpless coming to the realization *that I probably won't be going to my sister's wedding,* when Momma throws open my door?

With a scowl on her face, her voice dripping with disgust she says, "Audrey Rose, get dressed your Grandparents should be here any minute to get you. I'm letting you go to your sister's wedding. Don't think it's because your Grandmother has anything to do with it. I just don't want to have to put up with your sulking around and blaming me for this, so hurry they're running late."

Dragging the hem of my blouse across my face to wipe the tears I cry, "Thank you, Momma, this will mean a lot to Ceely and me. Momma, can I take Cossette and Craig?" I knew I was pushing it, but I have to ask.

Walking toward the door, she stops slightly turns her head to look at me over her shoulder. With a coldness in her eyes, I have never seen before she says, "No, absolutely not! Your sister has disrespected your Father, and you have chosen to disrespect me. I will not tolerate you including the rest of the family in this." With that said she was gone.

For a split second I thought about not going, *only a flash of guilt went through me*, then jumping up I run to the closet and throw on a dress Ceely had given me before she moved. Standing in front of the mirror I frown, it doesn't look great, but this will have to do.

When we arrived at the wedding, it was beautiful. Everyone from Levi's family is here. No one, but Granddaddy, Grandmother and me are here from our side of the family. I feel bad for Ceely; with most of her family missing, but she looks just beautiful. For the reception, everyone is going back to Levi's Mother's house. It's nice too, and Victoria Rose is excited that everyone is taking her picture. She thinks this whole day is about her. That's my niece always the center of attention. Nothing is said about the absence of our family. They are married, and that's all that matters. I'm also happy because Parker is here.

Oh, let me backtrack a little. A couple of months before the wedding Ceely's TV broke, so she had sent it out to get repaired. On the day it was due back she ask if I could come over and wait for them to deliver it. Mom said yes, so Levi picked me up that morning. Craig, my little brother, wanted to go too so I took him with me. When Lee pulled in front of the house, we ran out but just as I was getting to the car a guy got out of the front seat and got into the back with Craig, so I jumped up front. Levi dropped us off at Donna's apartment and said he would see us later and thank me for coming over. Later that day after Ceely got home from work Levi came by to take Craig and me home. After joking with Craig and giving me a hard time, which he loves to do, Lee got serious and said he needed to ask me something.

With an impish smile, he says, "A friend of mine would like to go out with you Audie.

His name is Parker, and I think you would like him." He then winks at me.

I make a face at him and tell him no thank you, "Levi I've only dated twice, and both of them were friends of yours. No offense in your taste of friends, ah but no. Besides, why would this guy want to go out with me? He's never even met me."

I've learned to be cautious when dating Levi's friends. Guy's can be very narrow-minded. One guy, I dated that was Levi's friend thought I was ready to sleep with him just because my sister had a baby without being married. Well, he picked the wrong girl for that, after telling him what I thought about him and his ideas I told him to take me home. He said, but he loved me and that he would use protection. I told him there was no possible way he could have fallen in love with me in the little bit of time we had been together. Yes part of me, the dreamer side would have loved to believe him but as young as I was I knew better. He said I guess I picked the wrong sister. I was getting upset by then. I was so tempted to jump out of the car and tell Levi what he was saying. We were at the Drive-In movies and Ceely, and Levi is parked next to us.

I decided real quickly that I can handle this. I scoot even closer to the door. With one hand on the door handle just in case I need to run and with all the maturity I could muster, I say to my date,

"Just because my sister has a baby, and isn't married to the jerk doesn't mean she is easy either. Her one and only mistake was trusting someone like you." Well needless to say he took me home, and I never heard from him again. I also never mentioned it to Ceely and Levi. I didn't want to upset them, besides I knew he wasn't that close of a friend to Levi.

Well, to make a long story short I went out with Parker a few days later. I knew right away he was different. Not that I had a lot of experience with guys, but as a person, he was very kind. We didn't do much but go to the local Dairy Queen and talk, well I mostly listened, but I felt a connection to him. Even though his life was worlds apart from mine, I knew this was the guy for me. We dated a couple of more times after that and then Parker joined the Air Force. Everyone was upset. They wanted me to talk him out of it, but I wasn't going to do this. I knew enough about him by now to know this was something he needed to do at this point in his life. I don't know why I had these feelings or thoughts, but even at 16, I knew this was a life-changing event in his life. Something that he wanted to do to help him grow as a man. It hurt I didn't want Parker to go either, but I know if I had a chance to change the direction of my life I wouldn't want anyone to stop me. So I supported him in his decision, besides Vietnam was going on and he had already received a Draft number. He said he would rather be in the air fighting the enemy than on the ground. It made sense to me, and I felt he had done enough soul searching to know what he needed and wanted to do.

Well as I said before, Parker is at the wedding. He is Levis' *best man*. After all the pictures have been taken at the reception, I go to find Parker. He is out front with the other guys in the wedding doing awful things to Levis' car. I walk up to him and ask if I can talk to him for a minute when they are through. He says sure. I need to find out why he hadn't called or came by when he said he would have the week before. I walk back into the house, and Ceely calls me over. I think, oh please no more pictures. Ceely has a serious look on her face and asks if I would help her change. We go into Levi's Mom's bedroom.

Ceely turns around and with that big sister, look says, "Audie I was afraid of this and didn't want you to be hurt. I could just kill Levi for setting you up with Parker. Sis, Parker is confused right now. He doesn't know what he wants to do, and the threat of going to Vietnam has messed him up. I wish you wouldn't see him anymore. He can't depend on, and you need someone who will love and take care of you."

I had no idea what she was talking about and from my point of view neither did she.

I look at her with doubt and say, "Ceely I know how Parker feels. He has told me all his fears. No one understands him like I do. He doesn't even know at this point if he has made the right choice, but why should that make me break up with him. He needs me, Ceely. I can't turn my back on him now nor do I want to."

"Audie, Levi and I know Parker a lot better than you do and believe me, this is killing me to tell you this. Parker has been seeing his old girlfriend." Ceely was slipping her dress over her head as she said this.

"Ceely, did you say Parker is seeing his old girlfriend?" She nodded her head, and I felt my heart sink. "Okay, I can handle this Ceely. I will talk to Parker. You just get beautiful for your new husband, or should I say *more beautiful* if that's possible." She is still giving me that big stern sister look as I turn and hurry out the door.

Fighting back the tears that make me feel weak I slip out the back door. I look up into the night sky and pray for strength. Okay, I know I can handle this. I just need to talk to Parker, and if it's this other girl he wants, then I guess it's over. I take a few deep breaths and walk back into the house through the kitchen. I could see Levi and Ceely were ready to go. Not that they were going very far for their honeymoon, just to the Holiday Inn Hotel, but we all needed to see them off. I go out front behind everyone and run up and gave them both a kiss.

"You two be happy. Y'all make a beautiful couple." Ceely has tears in her eyes. I tell her not to worry and have fun.

I stood for a long time after they had driven away, lost in thought. I feel my arm being pulled more than seeing. Victoria Rose is doing a dance at my feet for me to pick her up. She looks confused. I'm sure she doesn't understand any of this. I reach down and lift her, and give her a kiss on the cheek.

"Hey sweetie, you sure look beautiful today. Mommy and Daddy will be back tomorrow and tonight you get to stay with Memaw. How exciting is that? How about we go get some cake?"

That made her happy. Everyone calls Levi's Momma Memaw. Victoria is a lucky little girl,l for Ceely to find a family like this to love her. As we near the porch, Parker walks up. Either I was looking at him different or there is something sad about him tonight.

"Hi sorry it took me so long. Do you think we could take a ride? I will take you home." He was smiling and playing with Victoria.

"Sure let me call Momma and tell Grandmother. Will you take Victoria for some cake." I look back as I walk away, and a thought came to me. *I'm going to miss him.*

Momma gave me a hard time, but she finally said yes and not to be late. Grandmother was a whole different story. She didn't approve. I should be going with them not some boy. It's disrespectful, and she thought that boy should come and ask Granddaddy's permission.

"Grandmother Parker and I have been dating for awhile. Momma said it is okay. She has met him, and I would never do anything to disrespect you." I say this with a kiss upon her cheek.

I see the softness return to her eye's. My Grandmother is like a Momma tiger when it comes to her Grandchildren. She just grunts at me and says for me to stay on my side of the car and gave me a dime to put in my shoe if I needed to call them. How funny people can be? Parker, I can handle, it's the other men in my life I have no control. Protect me from them Grandmother; please protect me from them.

Parker and I drove out to Tripp Road. This road is a very isolated street in Mesquite where the wild boys like to come to race their cars, Parker being one of them, and it is also considered to be Lovers Lane for all the popular Mesquite kids. I don't know too much about that world because I've never been popular or part of The In Crowd. I never really needed that in my life, nor would that crowd ever consider letting me in. Thank goodness, though; tonight no one is here. I'm relieved because we need to talk without being interrupted.

As soon as he turns out the lights, Parker takes my hand and urges me to move closer toward him. I scoot a little closer but then stop. He is staring at me with a gentle smile on his face. That's one of the things that attracted me to him, his smile. In my eye's he can do no wrong when he smiles like that. He has the type of smile that is contagious. You would just have to smile back. He kisses as he smiles. It is so soft and gentle, never hard or demanding. It is as if he knew he had to go slow with me. That's the Parker I know. He doesn't have to prove he is a big and tough guy with me like he does for the rest of the world. All his friends call him *Little Bastard* and well deserved I've told. I know I see a side of Parker that he doesn't let anyone else see, except maybe his Momma. I know the sun rose and set on him for her. He is her *baby boy*. I never met a guy or anyone for that matter which is as honest as he is either. He once told me he would never tell me he loved me unless he meant it, and he hasn't. I respect him for that. I know he's not perfect, but in my heart what he stands for is pretty close to it.

I pull my eyes from him, and when he starts to kiss me, I backed away and said, "Parker we need to talk."

"Oh no am I getting a *Dear John* letter before I even leave?" He said this jokingly, but I could see the sadness in his eyes.

"No, I would never do that to anyone. It isn't about me; it's about you and what you want or should I say need. Please just let me get this out before you say anything." My voice is breaking as it always does when I have to say something that I know is going to hurt.

"I want to find out why you didn't call me, and you didn't show up for our date last Saturday. Is it because you're seeing your old girlfriend, so I've been told. What I need to know now Parker is where I stand with you. Parker, I won't be one of many girls in your life. I have to be the only one, and if your old girlfriend gives you what you need, then you need to stay with her." I look up to stop the tears that are threatening to fall and clear my voice. Parker is looking at me with understanding written all over his face. He doesn't try to stop me, so I went on.

"Believe me; I know how mixed up you are now. I know your feelings and thoughts are being pulled in a hundred directions, but Parker I also have to protect myself. You once told me you wouldn't tell me that you loved me until you were sure. Well, I think I'm falling in love with you, no I am falling in love with you, and I don't think you can answer honestly about how you feel right now, nor do I want you too. I think you need some time alone to think about your life without having to worry about a relationship too." I turn and look out the window into the darkness to hide my tears. It's killing me, but I know it is the best for both of us.

"Can I talk now?" He says this as he reaches for my hand. I just nod.

"You once told me that I was the most honest person you've ever met. Of course, they're some people who would disagree with you, but let me be totally honest with you now. I have never met a girl who was as wise as you. I mean you're sixteen, and you know me better than I do. You see a side of me that I have never seen, but more astonishing than that is your maturity. All the girls I have dated just want to have fun and yes I have hurt a few not caring about their feelings, but Audrey you're different. I've known that from the beginning, and I don't want to hurt you." He is looking into my eyes as he says this and at that moment a feeling came over me. I felt like I was listening to my best friend and that was okay.

"Now to answer your question. I know I should have called you and I didn't. I know now just how wrong that I was. A buddy of mine came by, and we went out, and before I knew it, it was 2:00 in the morning. I know that's no excuse, but I am sorry. Maybe I do need some time alone. I would never hurt you intentionally, but I also know right now I tend to think of no one but me." He turns the steering wheel and starts the car.

We drove all the way to my house in silence. When he pulls up to my driveway, he takes my hand. "Audrey, I do care about you. Please give me a second chance. I leave next week, and I don't want to leave with you mad at me. Can I call you tomorrow and maybe go somewhere on Tuesday before I leave? He sounded like a *little lost puppy.*

"Yes, Parker call me tomorrow. Make it after five though I have to work." Then he kisses and gives me a strong hug like he is afraid to let go.

Parker did call the next day, and we made plans to go out Tuesday night, but he never showed up. I waited and waited by the phone for his call. I just know something has happened to him. Finally, I give up and go to bed. I don't think my heart has ever hurt this bad. I know then just how much I love him. In my mind, I was making up all kinds of excuses for why he was treating me this way, but in the end, I knew I had to let go. I tell myself that he does care, but he is scared. I understand that, but I'm not going to let myself ever get hurt like this again. I cry like I have never cried before. When my tears subside I decide right then, I'm never going to get married. I will just get a better job after I graduate and get an apartment. I will never depend on anyone for anything. I hate this feeling it is worse than being hurt physically. I feel like I've lost a piece of my heart. Someone reached in and took it, and I know if Parker never comes back to me I will never be able to get it back. That's just fine I told myself. I don't need him or anyone. The last thought that came into my head was *I feel so lonely.*

The next morning Carmen rushed into my room and said Parker is on the phone, "Sis, C'mon get up it's Parker."

I opened my eyes, and they feel like sandpaper. "Carmen, I don't want to talk to him. Tell him, Oh; I don't care what you tell him. I don't feel like talking to anyone right now."

Carmen gave me an exasperating look and said, "Audie don't be that way. I know you still care for Parker. Just look at your eyes, and guys can be this way sometimes, c'mon talk to him."

I rise up on one arm and look at Carmen and shake my head. "Carmen, guys, may do this to other girls, but it's not going to happen again to me. Tell him I said to be careful and maybe we can talk when he gets back, but not now."

Carmen just shook her head and went back out into the hallway. I heard her tell him that I wasn't ready to talk to him. She said she was sorry and then told him maybe he could call back later. Carmen came back into my room and sat on the bed. She lovingly pats my hair. That's all it took. I sit up and start crying all over again. I feel my whole world crashing around me. Everything bad that has ever happened to me is ricocheting all through my head.

I'm crying to Carmen that I don't want to live anymore, "I'm tired of getting knocked down. I don't have any more fight in me. Carmen, I pray and pray, but I still get hurt. I try so hard not to hurt anyone, and I always end up getting hurt myself. Well, I'm through, Carmen. I'm not doing this anymore. From here on out I'm only going to worry about, *Me.*"

I didn't realize that I was screaming until the door opened and Freddy asks what is going on. I look up at him and yell as mean as I can, "You get out of my room. Don't ever come in here again. *Just leave!*" The look on his face was threatening.

I knew I had gone too far, but at that moment I didn't care. Carmen got up and slowly pushed him out into the hallway. I hear her tell him just to let her handle it and that she would explain later. Freddy listened to her and walked away without a word. Funny I thought, I guess men don't know how to handle a girl when she's mad, or maybe they just don't want to. That is the Carmen I know. This is my big sister who we all looked up to, as we should our mother. At this moment Carmen could have been married to a thousand Freddy's, and I couldn't have loved her more. She came back and told me to scoot over. She lay down on the bed with me and hugs me.

We lay there for a long time before either one of us speaks.

Carmen breaks the silence, "Hey little sister are you okay now? Can we talk?"

"Yeah, I will be okay. Thanks Carmen for being here for me. I'm sorry I lost it for a while there. I didn't mean to hurt Freddy. Well yes, I did. I mean, oh you know what I mean don't you?" I didn't feel bad that I yelled at Freddy, but I didn't want to hurt Carmen by yelling at her husband.

"I know sis; sometimes I want to yell at him too. I know this also seems like the end of your world but believe me it's not. When I lost Robin, I just wanted to die. You remember Robin, don't you? Of course, you do. Rather you can understand this or not. I do love Freddy, Audie. Yes, there are times I wish it could be different, but it's not. You know Daddy always drummed into our heads that God has a plan for us, and he does. We have to believe that, Audie. Look he gave me two beautiful sons. There's a reason for everything. You will love again; you're still young." Carmen stops when I go to open my mouth in protest.

She then goes on to say, "No I'm not saying you don't know what love is. You do. It's just that honey you've never really dated. It's strange I know, but Momma has sheltered you. I will tell you this *you are stronger than I could ever be*. I don't think I would have had the strength not to jump on that phone if a guy called to apologize to me. Don't write Parker off Audie. He does care for you. Don't ask me how I know I just do." She stops and gives me a hug.

"Thanks, sis. I do feel better, but I still don't want to talk to Parker. Carmen, I love you." I walk over and hug my big sister. No, I hold on to her for dear life. I don't want to let go. I want it to be like this forever.

She let go of me and laughed, "Audie, you know I love you too. No matter what ever happens just know that I will always be here for you." As she turns and walks out of the room my tears fall again, but this time they are tears of love for my big sister.

Chapter 16

The woman's decisions will protect the child.
The woman's faith is strong and alive.
She will no longer feel the pain of the child.

Carmen is so upset with me. Parker has been gone for three months and has written me just about every day. I haven't read any of his letters. When he first started writing, I told Carmen she could read them, but don't tell me what they said. She tried, though. She told me how sorry he was and that he thought he didn't deserve someone like me. I told her he's right he doesn't. She would get so upset and walk out on me.

One day almost four months later she came into my room and said, "Audie, you have to read this one. If you never read any of them read this one."

I rolled my eyes and told her to hand it over and leave the room. She was all smiles as she quietly closed my door. I slowly opened the envelope. Parker had such beautiful handwriting. I let my eyes soak in the words before I read them. I miss him a lot I thought. I propped my head up on my pillow and began to read.

Dear Audrey,

I miss you and hope to see you soon. I take it that you're still mad at me because you haven't written since I left. Audrey, I know I messed up bad. I took you for granted. I'm so very sorry. Please tell me you will forgive me. If not just know that I care about you still. I've got my head on straight now, and I am coming home for a visit in two weeks. If when I get home, you tell me to buzz off I will understand. I will never bother you again. I know I don't even have the right to ask, but please give me a chance to explain.

The rest of the letter was a blur. All I can think of is Parker is coming home and wants to see me. Every emotion is going through my body. I tell myself to calm down and think. I tend to think with my heart first. That's why I didn't read Parker's letters from the beginning. My heart is already forgiving him. Oh, I could just strangle my big sister. Okay, I told myself it wouldn't hurt to listen to what he had to say. I can be strong, as long as I didn't look at him. Oh, this will be disastrous. Maybe I should just write and tell him not to call me that it's over. No, he won't get the letter in time. Gosh, who am I fooling I want to see him too? *Okay, Audie just is strong and talk to him.* I told myself. Yes, that's what I will do. I will try to keep a cool head and listen to what he has to say and then decide. When I walk out of the bedroom, I almost trip over Carmen.

She is looking at me with her arms crossed, "Well? " she said.

I just shrug and walk past her. Knowing she is dying to know what I was going to do. I thought I would let her suffer a little bit but then felt bad, because I knew she just wants me to be happy.

"Okay Carmen, I'm going to see him and give him a chance to explain," I say this as I keep walking toward the kitchen.

She grabbed my arm and sat me in a chair and says, "Okay little sister tell me everything. I just read the first paragraph."

"Oh Carmen, the letter was sweet. I feel bad all these months not reading any of the letters." Before I could get another word in she is waving her hands in the air.

"Oh, he deserved it, but tell me how you feel. Have your feelings for him changed?" Showing this much excitement isn't like Carmen; she's usually calm and collective.

"Carmen, my feelings for Parker have never changed. I have always known I loved him, but he hurt me. Carmen, I can't let myself be hurt again. I will talk to him, but I still don't know if I can trust him. We'll see how it goes." I stood to leave, and she touched my arm.

"Remember Audie real love is hard to find and it doesn't come without a fight." With that, she walks off to pick up Heath, my nephew, from his playpen.

I sit there for a moment thinking how much I love her, and lucky I was to have her for a big sister. Carmen will never know how much I learned from her during this time and how much of my respect she has gained. Carmen isn't just my big sister. She is also a mother to all of us kids. I know some of the decisions Carmen made aren't right, but she has made them for all the right reasons. I've always thought my big sister is quiet and meek, but now I know different. She just knows which battles are worth fighting for, and thank goodness I was *that* battle this time.

Parker came home the following week. When he called I was so nervous; my voice shook when I answered. I f there was nothing else we had in common we could always communicate well, but this time, I was at a loss for words. He asked if he could pick me in about an hour. I said of course. All the while my legs are shaking and I feel dizzy. I think I changed clothes fifteen times, not that I had that many outfits, it just felt like it.

I was in the bathroom brushing my hair, and Carmen popped her head in and said, "Sis, Parker's hear. Oh, come on you look beautiful, and Audrey be nice okay?

I give her my most sophisticated look and say, "Carmen, you know I am always nice to the guy's I date. It's the ones that hurt me who are in trouble."

She just laughs and pulls my hair, "Oh yes, I forgot you're such a woman of the world. Well, c'mon Cleopatra your chariot awaits you."

We both laugh, and I follow her into the living room. Parker is sitting on the couch talking to, of all people, Freddy. The happiness I felt vanishes. I know Carmen can feel me stiffen. She gives me a little push into the room. Parker and Freddy both look up as we enter.

Parker stands and walks over to me and takes my hand. I'm still watching Freddy. Wondering, *what has Freddy been saying to Parker.* All I can think of is my wonderful day had just ended before it had started.

Parker's voice breaks the silence, "Are you ready to go?" He then turns to Freddy and asks, "It will probably be late before we get home is that okay?"

Before I can open my mouth in protest, Freddy walks over and pat's Parker on the back and says no problem but to be home by midnight.

Freddy then turns to me and attempts to take my hand. I pull it away. He then says with that irritating grin of his, "Now Audie, you be a good girl. Y'all don't do anything I wouldn't do."

I was trying hard not to say something that would embarrass Carmen and at the same time not to let Parker know just how disgusting Freddy is to me. It takes all I have to turn and walk out the door with Parker without turning back and making a face at Freddy. A wonderful feeling comes over me, though, as I walk to Parker's car with him. The closer I get to Parker's car, and the further my house is behind me I feel safe. I feel as if I have the wings of an Angel on my back guiding me and lifting all the pain, and anger that had been weighing me down.

Parker and I drove to his house and had dinner with his parents. I like his parents. They are so down to earth. His Mother and Dad always made me feel part of the family, but this time, it was different I think they were happy I was there with Parker. Not that anything was said, but I could feel it. After dinner, Parker and I drove to our favorite place to be alone and talk. He turns off the engine and puts the keys in his pocket. I'm looking at him wondering what he did that for, but before I could ask he turns toward me and smiles.

With his right hand, he brushed my hair from my face and said, "Thanks for seeing me Audrey, and thanks for not hanging up on me when I called. You had every right to I know, but I was hoping you hadn't given up on me yet. You once told me *you didn't give your heart lightly to anyone,* and I was counting on that. When you didn't answer any of my letters, I almost gave up, but something inside me told me not to. Besides that, I talked about you all the time to my roommate in the barracks, and he told me I was an idiot if I let you get away. My Mom and Dad said the same thing. I talked to my Mom, and she said you were different than any girl I had ever dated. She said she could tell that you cared a lot for me. That you had seen the good and bad in me and yet you still loved me. Believe me; that means a lot coming from my Momma." He stops and looks a little embarrassed admitting he had asked his Momma for advice.

It did make me feel good because I thought his family might think I was just white trash and wouldn't want their son with me. I tried very hard to show them I wasn't the picture that society had painted me to be just because I come from a poor family. I also know that his Mother isn't that type of person, but this is her little boy who has been hurt very badly by his last girlfriend. I know she will go to the ends of the earth to protect him, and I respect her for that. Oh, it hurts to think that I may be thought of that way and judged by another's family this way, but I also understood there are parents out there that protected their children no matter what age they are.

My thoughts were interrupted when Parker reaches over and takes my hand. He says, "Audrey, I can't promise you being with me will be easy. I can't promise you that I won't do something to upset you again. But I will promise you this if you let me I will build your trust in me. I don't ever want to be without you again. I admit I am scared to love Audrey. I have been hurt badly by my last girlfriend, and it's hard for me to trust another girl not to hurt me again. I know now this wasn't fair to you. I didn't give you a chance. I just judged you on how she treated me. I thought you were too good to be true and that you would just hurt me too. Of course, you proved me wrong, all most to the point of losing you. Well, I guess that's all I can say. I know it's not enough, but I hope you still feel I'm worth fighting for." I was looking down at his hands while he had been talking. Somehow I knew this took everything he had to admit to me. Parker was a very quiet guy, and he didn't open himself up easily.

I had started to cry and through the tears, I say, "Parker I love you, and I'm afraid too. I've never loved anyone before, except my family. It's all new for me, and I don't know how it's supposed to go or if there are rules to be followed. All I know is to follow my heart, and I am afraid of it getting broken again, but I'm more afraid of losing you." He didn't let me finish. He just grabbed me and told me not to cry and that he didn't ever want to be the reason for my tears again. He then kissed me, and I knew we were doing the right thing. This is our destiny. No matter what happens or against all odds, I will fight to stay with him.

The most beautiful thing that came from this whole ordeal is that Parker realized he loved me, and he told me so. He said I taught him a hard lesson. He knew that he had a lot of proving to do to me and that he would respect my wishes and take it slow. Parker went back to Minot, North Dakota. That's where they sent him to after Boot Camp. We write each other every day. Carmen laughs and says she can't even imagine what we would have to talk about, but she was happy for me.

Parker had been gone a month when he wrote and asked me to marry him. It threw me for a loop; I wasn't expecting it. I was saving my money to get an apartment so that I could move out of my mother's house and start my life after graduation. I didn't know what to do I loved him, but I didn't think I was ready to get married. I talked to Ceely and of course, she tried to protect me. She said she didn't think Parker was ready. She thought he was just lonely, and that was no reason to get married. I talked to Carmen, and she told me to follow my heart. She said there were no guarantees in life, but if I truly loved Parker then marry him. I felt more confused now than when he asked me. I knew to some extent Ceely was right, but I also knew Parker wouldn't have asked me to marry him, out of loneliness. I know he had done some heavy thinking and talking to his parents before he came to this decision. Carmen is right I do love him.

Oh my gosh, why am I even thinking twice about this? I know I want to spend the rest of my life with Parker. I want to have his baby and raise that beautiful family I have always wanted. Still, a part of me is scared. A part of me knows I will have to leave my brothers and sisters. I worry about leaving the little ones, but I know Carmen and Ceely will still be here. The only one I truly am worried about leaving was Cossette, but I also know how tough she is.

Freddy won't hurt her. Cossette won't let him. She is like Ceely. Strong willed nobody messed with her more than once. Junior is with Daddy, and he seems happy, and Craig is Momma's pride and joy. She won't let anything happen to him.

I get out my paper and pen and proceed to write Parker an answer. My hand shakes as I write. I tell him he has taken me by surprise and that I'm sorry that it has taken so long for me to write back with an answer. I tell him I love him, but there were some thing's I had to work out within me before I could give him an honest answer. Then I wrote. *Yes, Parker, I will marry you.* I'm not afraid of my love for you anymore, and I know that you are my destiny. No matter what anyone says, we are meant to be together. As I write, I feel confidence in my decision come over me. For the first time in my life, I'm going to be happy and have control.

My Aunt Reba came by today and said she would like to talk to me. As usual, she was very blunt and up front with her feelings.

She says, "Audrey if you're just marrying Parker to get out of your mother's house you better think twice. A husband is ten times worse than a parent can be and he will expect a lot more from you. Have you talked to your Mom about what it takes to be a wife? I can't believe she is letting you do this." I just wanted to laugh. I knew my Aunt Reba was not as naive as she sounded. I should have expected this. I'm sure Momma put her up to talking to me.

She knew I loved Aunt Reba, but what she didn't know was that I felt Aunt Jean had never had control of her life, and I wouldn't let her have an impact on mine, but as usual for me, I would be polite and listen to the advice she had for me. I also knew Aunt Reba and Momma were like two peas in a pod yet worlds apart.

"Aunt Reba I'm not marrying Parker to get away from Momma. I love Momma. No, I don't like the things Momma does, but I love my Mother. Yes, I talked to her about marrying Parker, but I don't need her advice on what it takes to be a wife. Momma told me I could marry Parker, but I couldn't leave with him. We plan to get married in June, and I will be going to North Dakota where he is stationed at Minot AFB. I told her I would be eighteen in August, and if we have to, we will just wait until then to get married. Aunt Reba that was Momma's advice to me." I could see Aunt Reba was getting frustrated with me.

"Okay Audrey, it sounds like you have made up your mind. It doesn't matter how the family feels. I just want you to know I don't give your marriage a year, and you will come crying back to your Momma. Just remember once you leave home it's never the same when you come back." I thought that was kind of funny thing to say. I wonder if I did come back, which I knew I wouldn't, but if I did, would the change she's talking about be better because I couldn't see how it could get worse.

Well, Momma gave in, and Parker and I are married on June 10th, 1971. I feel like the luckiest girl in the world. It was a small ceremony, but it was beautiful. My Daddy gave me away. I couldn't have been more proud. All the people I loved were there. Now as we get ready to leave, I am sad. I guess in the months before the wedding I never really thought about having to move away. Now it is hitting me like a ton of bricks. My sisters have tears in their eyes. *Oh no, now I am crying too.* I hugged each one them and realized we were going to be separated for the first time in our lives. Parker keeps saying we will be home for visits and that we will call. That doesn't seem to make a difference. He will never realize the bond we share and how scared we all are in this change in our lives. I walked over to Junior to kiss him. He grabbed me and held on like I did with Carmen that day in my bedroom. Oh, I can't do this I thought.

He said, "Audrey, I'm going to miss you so much. Don't go."

"Junior I have to. I'm married now. You can come and visit. It's not like I'm leaving forever, and I promise to call." I start to cry now.

Junior let go of me and said, "Audie I don't even know where Minot, North Dakota is. You might as well be on the moon. Nothing will be the same anymore." I had never expected Junior to take me leaving this hard.

Momma broke the tension and said, "Okay let your sister go and let's get one more picture. Okay, that's good now Audie kiss Parker. Okay, done."

I was so embarrassed I had never kissed a boy in front of my Momma. It just felt wrong. Parker and I got into the car and backed out of the driveway. I knew Junior was right things would never be the same again. Is my love for Parker strong enough to get me through leaving my family? As Carmen said, there were no guarantees. I shook my head to clear my thoughts. I know it is a little too late to worry about these things now. Parker reaches over and takes my hand and says it will be okay. Yes, I'm doing the right thing, I thought.

Everything will be all right as long as I'm sitting next to Parker. I turn around to wave goodbye again, and the last person I see is Freddy standing next to Momma.

I know then, as we got further away, I wasn't just leaving my family behind I was leaving the bad memories too. I decided I am starting a new life, and there will be no room for sad thoughts. I not only feel that this is where God wants me, but he has guided me here all along. I know from the minute I met Parker he is my *Night in Shining Armor*. Now as Dallas, Texas fades behind me I have no doubts or fears. The bad memories have been successfully tucked away!

Chapter 17

She now lives with love and writes with Gods pen.
He carries her pain within.
She now knows the child did not sin.

Here I sit 32 years later as I put pen to paper and write my final chapters. I realize how blessed I am to be free. I also realize how naïve I was at seventeen to believe by driving away from the people who had hurt me the most, would wash away the bad memories never to surface again. I thought I had won. I had found a way to survive and in my mind all those years I had. I didn't realize that the day that I drove back home to Dallas, my home that I had left so many years before, that those memories would still be waiting for me. Just waiting for me to let them in, *and let them in I did.* Not purposely, no it was a slow process. Memories that took ten years to surface after I returned. I know God wanted me back in Dallas. I know He has work he needs me to finish there. I just didn't know the price I would have to pay to carry out his plan for me.

My main reason for returning was to help take care of my Grandmother. Two years ago she had been diagnosed with Alzheimer's. My Granddaddy needs help with her, not that he will admit or ask for help, but I will be there for them. I also know that Ceely can't do this alone either, and Mom had moved back to Arizona with Carmen and Freddy 20 years before. She had already made it clear she wouldn't move back to Dallas, so because of a series of mysterious circumstances we decided to come home.

If someone would have asked me the year before, if I would ever think of moving back to Dallas I would have said no. I was a Manager for the Army and Air Force Exchange Service. I had been with this company for over fifteen years. Parker had his own Aviation Business. We had bought a home in California City, California. Not far from Edwards Air Force Base where Parker had recently retired from the Air Force and started his own business. My son had just graduated from High School and joined the Air Force, and my oldest daughter was due to graduate that year. My youngest daughter was in the eighth grade. Our life was going strong, and there was nothing to make me think that it would completely change within a year, but it did. Everything seemed to start slowly falling apart. The people who Parker had trusted to go into business with walked out on him with more than just their briefcases, so we had to take a loss and close down his business. We not only lost the business, but we would end up losing our home too. I kept telling him it would be okay he would find something else. We still had my job, but things didn't get better. The Aviation field in California started failing. Parker couldn't find work anywhere unless he accepted a job out of town. That would mean having to live apart from the kids and me, and we didn't want that. Parker had missed so much of our children's younger years, being in the military. In his field of expertise, they had to deploy a lot. He promised this would not happen once he retired, so we lived on my paycheck as long as we could. During this time my job had sent me to a seminar in Dallas. While I was there, I spent two days with my Grandparents. That's when I noticed Grandmother had gotten worse. Granddaddy told me he wished I would come home. The day I left my Grandparents cried. It broke my heart to drive away from them, again. When I got back to California things hadn't changed. Parker still couldn't find work in his field. I told him about Grandmother and how sick she was getting. He said to me, then let's go home. He said there was nothing left for us here, so I put in my notice and within a month we were going home. We left California and everything we had built two weeks after our oldest daughter graduated.

For the next four years, it was hard, but Parker and I were able to find work. Our lifestyle was totally different from what we were used to, but at least I was home again and could be there for my Grandparents as they were for me when I was little. It was hard trying to help Granddaddy with Grandmother and hold down a job, but I did, for a while. Then in our fifth year home, Grandmother took a turn for the worst. I knew I was going to have to get professional help for her, so I called the Alzheimer's Association, and they said I needed to get her evaluated through St. Paul's Geriatric Clinic of Dallas. It was hard to get her an appointment with them because they only allowed new patients very rarely. There was such a demand for their services that they usually only took patients from family members who had been clients before. I begged them to take Grandmother. I told them I didn't know what else to do. My Grandmother had recently gotten out of the hospital from open-heart surgery, and before that she had fallen trying to help my Granddaddy out of bed and had broken her collarbone. My Granddaddy had refused to believe my Grandmother had Alzheimer's disease even though she had been diagnosed in 1985 when she was sixty-nine years old. When Grandmother had her heart attack, Granddaddy didn't call me until the day after when she was in the middle of her second attack. The doctor said she had severely damaged her arteries and that we were lucky she was alive. I finally convinced St. Paul to take her. They gave me the only appointment they had open, and that was three months away. I didn't care. Finally, I was going to have help for her. I knew very little about this disease they called Alzheimer's. I knew my Grandmother would eventually lose her short-term memory, but I was not prepared for the devastation that this disease would do to my Grandmother, or me. No, I wasn't prepared at all. Over the next two years, I regularly took my

Grandmother to the Clinic for check-ups. I threw myself into learning everything I could about the disease. Little did I know then that the most important thing I needed to learn I didn't find in any of the books or tapes I studied. Oh, it was there for me to read, but I didn't think it was important so I would just discard the warnings and only read about the disease and how to help Grandmother. All the information on Care Givers and how important it was for them to take care of themselves, I just tossed.

How naïve of me to think I didn't need help, after all, it was Grandmother who needed me. I was healthy I could do this. I never once thought about the toll it would take on my family or me. Oh, how wrong I was. I let it consume me before I realized I was hurting Grandmother and Granddaddy by not getting help. I was either at work or with my Grandparents. It got where I would no more get home from work and Granddaddy would call with another emergency with Grandmother, so eventually, I had to quit working. Granddaddy got where he fought me the whole way. Sometimes I would have to lie to him and say I was taking her to lunch or the grocery store just to get her to St.

Paul. The doctors at St. Paul were telling me I needed to put Grandmother in a Nursing Home for her on safety and mine. I just couldn't think of that. No, I would do anything to keep her out of one of those Homes, besides Granddaddy would never let me do that. Granddaddy was ten years older than Grandmother, by then he was 92. Then my worst nightmare happened. I realized something was wrong with my Granddaddy's too. He took to his bed and wouldn't get up. I counted on him to help me with Grandmother and up until then, he did. He would call when she tried to wander off or if she hurt herself. I knew he was changing and getting more demanding and not trusting people. He wouldn't even let my sister Ceely come to his house to help me, as a matter of fact, I was the only one he would let come in, besides the occasional nurse that Medicare lets me hire to help with him and Grandmother.

Ceely and I finally called Adult protection services in to help us with Granddaddy. We were so afraid he was going to hurt Grandmother. We knew how much he loved her. His very existence was for her, but he wasn't himself anymore. He was becoming dangerous. Well, the Adult Protection Services came out and told us unless Granddaddy gave them permission we couldn't take Grandmother out of the house. Not only that but because he was our step-Grandfather, we had no rights when it came to making decisions for him either. I had a power of Attorney for Grandmother. St.Paul made sure I got that in the very beginning, but not for Granddaddy. They said in the state of Texas as long as the husband was alive and hadn't been deemed by a doctor as losing his abilities to make decisions that we had no rights. While they were there, they went into the bedroom to talk to Granddaddy, and he told them to get out of his house. They packed up their briefcases and walked out saying they were sorry, but their hands were tied. Ceely and I sat there dumbfounded and cried. Twice Grandmother had turned the gas on the stove and forgot to light it. Luckily both times I had come over and smelled it when I walked in. We told the agency that but they still walked out. I had to call them out two more times after that, but still, they said they could do nothing. Finally, I was forced to call the police. It had been three weeks since I got Granddaddy out of bed. He developed bedsore on his back that turned infectious. I couldn't get him to a doctor, so I called St. Paul, they had even been out to talk to him, but he wouldn't listen to them either. He said everyone worked for the government and just wanted his money and house. St Paul said to try and see if I could get a doctor to come to the house and evaluate Granddaddy. I think it would have been easier to get the President of the United States to come and talk to him. Needless to say every doctor I called turned me down. They all said the same thing. Since my Grandmother had Alzheimer's, she couldn't have him removed either. We had to get him to come into the hospital on his on free will. They said otherwise I would have to call the police and tell them I thought he was a danger to society, and they would take him to Jail and then to Parkland Hospital to be evaluated. I couldn't believe it they wanted me to call the police on my 92-year-old sick Grandfather and put him in Jail. I think me and Ceely cried and prayed more that day than ever in our lives before. I called the Balch Springs police where my Grandparents lived and told them our situation they said they would come out that we couldn't leave our Grandparents if we thought they were a danger to the community. My mind was going in a hundred directions. I knew I had to do something and fast. My Granddaddy was going to die if I didn't get him help. Grandmother was in her world trying to get him to eat some soup that he just kept knocking out of hand, and telling her to go away and leave him alone. I got out the yellow pages and just started calling every professional place that dealt with emergencies. Finally after eight hours of waiting and still no police I called the Director of Ambulances in Dallas. I was desperate I knew I had to do something to get help for my Grandparents. Our fear of them was tearing Ceely and me apart. No Grandchild should ever have to go through this. After I had told three people my story, I was finally patched through to the Director. He told me to heck with bureaucracy he would send an Ambulance out there and get my Granddaddy to a Hospital. I could have kissed that man. Ceely and I went out and sat on the porch and waited. Within 30 minutes an Ambulance pulled up in front of my Grandparents house. Right behind them low and behold, the Balch Springs police. While the paramedics were trying to talk to Ceely and me, the police told me they needed a statement of what was going on. I told them if they had of been here eight hours ago when I first called them I might have had time to chit chat with them, but right now someone is here to help with my grandfather so his statement would have to wait. By this point, I didn't care if they arrested me. I knew all these people scared my Grandmother, and she needed me. When I got into the house, Ceely had Grandmother in the kitchen and was comforting her. The paramedics said they needed me in the bedroom with Granddaddy. I walked in expecting him to yell at me, but what I saw made me go weak in the knees.

He was holding his hand out reaching for me. He asked me who these people were and what had he done. I told him they were here to help him that the doctor sent them. They asked Granddaddy his name and what day it was, of course, he didn't have a clue how to answer either question. They said they were going to take him to the hospital and get him some help. Granddaddy said okay as long as I was with him. My heart was breaking, but I knew I had to be strong.

I wish I could say everything went smooth after that, but it didn't. Granddaddy went into the Nursing Home. We had to watch our strong Granddaddy lose what dignity he had left. Ceely and I tried so hard to make him think everything was okay and that he would go home soon. His main concern was my Grandmother. The worst part was having to lie to my Granddaddy, but I knew I had to and hoped God would forgive me. Ceely and I tried to take care of Grandmother at her home in Balch Springs. Ceely and my daughters helped as much as they could, but it was just too hard to split us between our homes and hers. Not to mention the damage it was doing to my body and mind. I tried to take Grandmother to live with me, but that didn't work either she kept trying to leave and walk home, so Ceely took her home with her, and that didn't work either. We finally had to give up and did what St. Paul tried to tell us to do in the beginning. Grandmother went to the Nursing Home. We had to lie to her too. We told her the doctors said Granddaddy needed her to be with him in the nursing home he had to go to. It weighed heavily on me that lying to my Grandparents was coming so easily to me, even though it was for all the right reasons. At first, we had them in the same room, but that got too dangerous for Grandmother. She still tried to take care of Granddaddy and kept getting hurt. We even hired private nurses to stay with them so they could stay together, but then we ran out of money, so we were forced to put them in separate rooms. When we had to sell their home, Ceely and I cried. We knew then we were saying goodbye to our grandparents forever. We took seventeen thousand dollars from the sale of the house and made funeral arrangements for both of them. We knew when the time came we wouldn't be able to do it emotionally, so we decided to take care of it then. One of the hardest but smartest things we did at that time.

Ceely and I also realized that *society* not only neglected to protect the children, but the elderly was on that list too. We felt like our society just looked at the Elderly as useless commodities, after all, they don't pay taxes, and when their savings has been used up, they become a burden on the State. Yes, I learned a lot about how people only care about you if you have money. Once my Grandparents savings had depleted and they had to go on Medicare, even the Nursing Homes treated them differently. I continuously had to go to the Nursing home and fight for my Grandparents rights. All we asked is that they treat them with dignity, but I guess we were asking for too much; after all, they were on Medicare now. It wasn't like my Grandparents didn't still pay. They took my Grandparents Social Security checks and my Granddaddy's retirement check, but I guess that wasn't enough for the Nursing Homes.

There was a Nursing Home we had them in that cared for their elderly patients, *Seago Manor* in *Seagoville, Texas*. The staff was so good to my Grandparents and us. *Seago Manor* was the first Nursing home we had them in after their savings ran out, so Medicare helped pay for their stay here. I wish we could have let them stay there, but it was just too far away from me. I also need to thank one other person who I know God sent to me at that time, *Roberta Flock of Birds*. She is a Medicaid Eligibility Worker for Dallas, TX. I don't know what I would have done without her. She was assigned to my Grandparents the day they had to go on Medicare for support, and she was there with me the day they died. I hope she knows how much her help means to families who have loved ones in Nursing Homes.

We lost our Granddaddy two years after he went into the Nursing Home on January the 12th, 2002. I knew he had held on that long for Grandmothers sake. He thought he was still taking care of her even though she had to come to him. By then he couldn't even get out of bed. He was 95 years old when he passed. Grandmother passed away two and half months ago, May 18th, 2004. She was 87. I thought putting her in a Nursing home would be the hardest thing I would ever have to do. I honestly thought I had come to terms with losing my Grandmother years before. Then I thought, the hardest thing I had to go through was the day I walked in, and she didn't know who I was, but no nothing prepared me for actually losing my Grandmother. The day she died, and I kissed her for the last time I realized I wanted her to wake up and tell me everything would be all right, that she would never leave me. I know it was a blessing for her and me because I couldn't stand to see her suffer anymore. I prayed so many nights for God to take her away to be with Granddaddy, but when it happened, I fell apart. I knew a part of me was going with her, but more importantly, a large part of her would always be with my children and me. That little girl that needed her Grandmothers love so much was scared, but I let her go, and I thank God every day that he brought me home to them. I thank him that he gave me these last ten years to share with two people who taught me so much. They gave me a reason to live when I was young. They taught me how important a parent's love is, but more importantly they gave me that love.

Some people looked at my grandmother as small and weak, but as a child, she was the strongest woman I knew, and after living with Alzheimer's with her I found out just how brave she was.

The most important thing about Alzheimer's for a Care Taker to know is it isn't the loved one who has the disease that suffers the most it's you, *The Care Taker*, especially if you are caring for someone you love. While taking care of my Grandmother all those years I had to let her relive the past that wasn't always happy for her or me. I learned things about her life that I could have gone to my grave not knowing. My Grandmother would have been horrified if she realized what she was revealing to me. In my Grandmothers day, things that happened in the past stayed in the past. You put them in a closet and locked the door, and woe is to the person that opened that door.

Well that person for me was my Grandmother with Alzheimer's. My grandmother only went to the third grade. She lost her mother at three years old and was raised by her older sister and father. At sixteen she was raped and became pregnant with my mother. My grandmother fought to keep her baby, and she won, but while she was in the hospital, her father had the surgeon give her a complete *hysterectomy* so she couldn't have more children. You have to realize this was in an age where to be pregnant and not married brought shame to the family name and the father's word was law. No matter what the circumstances were that led up to the pregnancy. My Great Grandfather loved his daughter, and he thought he was doing this for her on good. For years after my mothers' birth, someone was always trying to take my mother away from my grandmother, but she stood her ground. She was determined to raise her daughter no matter what the cost to her. My Grandmother met and married my Grandfather, who was ten years older than her, and someone her father didn't approve of, but she did it. The day my Grandfather died they had been married for 65 years. Even though it was hard at times to listen to I would live through it with her all over again, for her. I know my Grandmother had no idea she was saying these things to me. Oh my gosh, she would have died if she knew I knew any of this, but that's what you have do. You just let them talk. It's part of the disease scattered memories they're reliving. Not for your benefit, but for their own. They have to feel they still belong. That they haven't lost everything, so you just sit and listen. Never and I mean never argue or correct an Alzheimer's patient, even if you think you're helping them. You won't be; you will be traumatizing them more. I also learned a lot of why my mother looked at life the way she did, no it doesn't make it right, but I do understand her better. I know now to understand a person you have to know where they've come from. No, my Momma would have never told me any of these things either, so that's why I feel God led me back home. My family needed me. I have always been the peacemaker in our family now I know why.

Chapter 18

He takes my hand and the field I can see.
He hands me a flower. I am safe and free.
He shields my eyes, even though I can see.
God stands before me. He would never leave me.

I said this in the beginning, and I will say it again. Writing this book was the hardest thing I have ever had to face in my life. Not because of the ugly things I had to, not only relive, or also put down on paper. Not even having to accept that this was my history and where I come from. No, what makes this so hard is I know I have to do this right the first time. There will be no second chances, no chance to erase or take something back. Yes, this is the most important message I need to get across to those of us who have been abused as children. No matter the abuse we were forced to endure, whether it was mental or physical.

We do not have to keep our shame and heartache inside. We do not have to bear this burden alone or carry the blame. Tell the world. Tell anyone who will listen, but

above all tell yourself this is not your fault.
You did nothing to deserve this except love
and trust everyone involved.

My sole purpose for writing my memoirs
from childhood is to bring peace and
insight to all who have suffered abuse. I
want them to know that there is hope, and
they are never alone. Not for one minute. If
we feel alone, then we have chosen to feel
this way. It's *society* that puts rules on us. It's
society that judge's us. Why, because we
let them. There's not one of us who doesn't
have control of our lives. Yes someone
may hurt our bodies and minds, but it's the
choices we make afterward that make all
the difference. If you chose, for the rest of
your life, to blame the person who hurt you,
then you are choosing to continue letting
them have control of your life. Hatred and
anger carried in your heart is a heavy
burden to bear. Believe me, I know. From
the time I married and left home to the day
I came back I thought I had mastered the
art of overcoming my abuse, but was I ever
wrong. I didn't realize I had to face the truth
of who I was and where I came from before
I could forgive or heal. I thought by burying
all the hurt and pain, I could still love my
Momma and Daddy, what I don't accept

or let in can't hurt me. I was wrong. Oh, so wrong. All I did was prolong the pain and let those who hurt me hurt others that I loved. At my Daddy's funeral when I was 26 I felt empty, yet my heart was breaking for this man who was my Father. A man that was gentle and loving, but could be oh, so cruel. I asked myself how I could feel love and yet hate him at the same time. I didn't realize at the time, but this is when I started changing. I knew to continue with my life and my spiritual beliefs I was going to have to face the truth. I was going to have to understand my feelings for my father and what he did to me.

I'm not going to tell you that I had a light come on, and *wow there it is the answer.* No, it took me a few years of soul searching and communicating with my siblings to understand it wasn't just me having trouble understanding my feelings for Dad. They were too. Here is the answer that I realize I can live with to move forward.

I can love my Daddy, but also hate the sickness that made him do the things he did to me. Then, and only then was I able to let go and forgive him.

Closing one door only opened another nightmare, my Momma's involvement or should I say lack of involvement in our lives. I know this is going to seem shocking, but I never really knew that all of us kids had suffered in some form at the hands of my father. You see it was after my Father died, and I went searching for answers that my siblings and I ever spoke of our childhood. Some, to this day, will not completely admit or let go of our abuse at his and my Momma's hands.

While sharing memories of life with our Daddy brought on more questions, about our Mother. *Why didn't she save us? Why didn't she do something to stop him? Dear God, why did she bring Freddy into our lives?* The one memory we all agree on is, *The Vow of Silence*, our parents taught us to live by. We were told never to tell anyone what went on in our house, and my Momma enforced this *rule*! It's the memory I had to face when I moved home to Dallas, Texas. I had dealt with my feelings for Daddy; now I knew I had to deal with Mommas part in all this. That's why I believe God led me home. He knew I would never reach my destiny if I didn't face my entire past. I had to forgive and completely release the anger and hate, which even I didn't know I carried in my heart. Surprisingly or should I say knowingly He led me to the very place that saved me as a child, *my Grandparents house.*

From the minute they sheltered me in their arms to the day I had to send them *Home to be with God* I was saved. I realize now, the field of flowers, which I escaped to as a child, brought clarity and acceptance into my adult life. My Grandmother gave me the greatest gift a child could receive, the ability to forgive unconditionally. After all, my Mother is her daughter; who could help me understand my mother better than my Grandmother? It wasn't so much what my Grandmother said as it was her actions that spoke loud and clear. I've learned now that there are people in this world that just doesn't get the concept of what love is or how to give it. Unfortunately, my Mother is one of those people, and yet my *Grandmother* still loved *her little girl.* While Grandmother still had some memory left, Mother wasn't there. When Grandmother needed her daughter the most, I couldn't get Mother to come. My Grandmother forgave her and loved her unconditionally until the day *Alzheimers* took not only her mind but her life.

Now when someone asks me, how can I love my parents, I honestly and truthfully say, because the love I gave them as a child and now is pure. I have chosen to forgive my parents and give them an unconditional love that all children have for their parents. The only negative feeling I have for my parents is sorrow for them. Knowing they missed out on so much by not protecting and loving the six little gifts God gave them. Believe me, when I say it's not you who has to live or pay for what was done to you it's the person who chose hurt you. They are the ones who will have to look in the mirror every day. The day will come when that person will have to answer for the pain caused by them. All you are responsible for is the choices you make afterward. If you chose to let it eat away at your heart, then you will continue to suffer and maybe repeat on others the pain that had been inflicted on you.

To stop the cycle of pain is one of the true meanings behind my memoirs. I have taken the important things, good and bad, that I learned from my childhood, and used them to make my life worthy. I chose to make the wrong right and to see the good and carry it with me always. I choose not to be the parent my Mother and Father were. I take my strength from my mother and Grandmother. Even though my Mother abused the power she had, I saw, through her actions, that women did not have to bow down to a man or anyone. We were all equals in life and love. From my Father, I took from the good side of him. He taught me how to love others and be kind to everyone, but most important his belief in God to protect me mind, body, and spirit. I know it's hard for you to read my book and hear me say this about him, but when he was on his *meds*, he was a good and loving person. Out of the bad from both of them, and Freddy I chose *what not to do*, and how to protect and love my children.

The love, respect, and care I have given my husband and children are what define me as a wife and Mother. The love I have for God is what gave me my freedom to be who I am today. The only thing I ask of my children in return is to love God and to love, care and protect their children, our Grandchildren.

Chapter 19

Let all bitterness, wrath, anger, clamor, and evil
speaking is put away from you with all malice. And
be kind to one another, tenderhearted, forgiving
one another, even as God in Christ forgave you.
Ephesians 4:31-32

It's not like God didn't warn us. He sent His only son down to bring this message to us. I feel Jesus' walk was not only to wash away our sins so His Father could forgive us and love us, but he also gave us a preview of what we would face in life as true Christians. It's not like we have gone through life blindly. No, we will never know the sadness he faced, but believe me as Humans, and we are only human, we will feel his pain. I trusted Jesus when He told me at three that God wasn't ready for me yet and that he would protect me. I know because I feel God was preparing me for the road ahead. You would have thought being burned as a child was lesson enough, but it was nothing compared to the tribulations that were before me and still are. When my husband and I had to bury our third child, Amber Renee's twin, due to Crib Death, *God was there*. He lifted me off of my knees and put Angela in my arms, and I knew life had to go on. No, God doesn't create the bad things in our lives. We do by the choices we make, right or wrong. He cries right along with us and waits for us to reach for him. He never turns from us. Like a loving parent, he stands behind us to catch us when we fall and fall we will. Without Him in our lives, we are lost.

Our big mistake is thinking He put others here to help us bear the burdens we go through, but boy was we wrong. *Only God* can pull us through our sorrows. *Only God* has the shoulders wide enough to carry us. Just never forget why Jesus chose to sacrifice himself for us. If you can fall back on Him in hard times, then there isn't anything you can't face, because you will never be alone. I know I am doing this for God. This is my purpose in life. All God asks of us is to love Him and each other, it's that simple. I knew at a very young age that no matter what happens to me throughout my life He was there and would always be. He made me that promise at three years old, and even though I never talked about what I had seen I carried His words with me and held Him to his promise. This book is my way of giving him thanks and love. I am blessed that I let him into my heart. Even when I thought I was alone, deep down, knew I wasn't. He gave me that security. Even when I had made wrong choices He was there, in the end, to pick me up, and demand that I do it right this time. I now know at an early age he instilled in me to love my parents, *for they know not what they do*. How else can I explain why I have never blamed them for my childhood, or why I still love them with all my heart? I believe in Gods fate. He has a plan for us all. Yes as His children we shake our heads and think we know better. We think how can He know what's best for us. He's not here seeing what we are going through, but then He jerks us out of our self-center ness. Then in ways we will never understand, He shows us that he has been with us all along.

I wish I could say that I have a line to God, but I don't. I wish I could say I will never have to face sadness again, but I will. I am now. My son is in the Marines now and is on his way back to Iraq again. My first instinct as a mother was to be mad. How dare they do this? It's not fair, and then

I turned to God. I begged Him not to let them send my son again. He may not make it back this time.

Please Dear Lord; don't let me lose another child, not like this. Not to a senseless War!

Then it happened God jerked me back to His reality. After praying, peace came over me. Who was I to judge Him now? Of course, He has a plan. I need to trust Him in no matter what happens it was meant to be. There is a reason my son needs to be there, and it isn't up to me to question, but that doesn't mean I'm not still mad and afraid. I just know I have to put my son in the hands of God and trust Him.

Please believe me when I say everything in my book is a true recollection of my childhood and the things I went through. I didn't write this to hurt anyone or for anyone to feel sorry for me. I wrote this book *from my heart.* If I can help one person, then I know all I have gone through to get this written and published was worth the pain. I know if I can make it through the life I have had then so can you. No matter what your pain is, or how you think Society will judge you, in the end, it's your choices that make all the difference. Have you ever really thought about who this group is that we've labeled, Our Society? Well, they are you and me, so when you point that finger to blame your mistakes on Society just remember you are a part of that group. The difference will be if you take control and point that finger at yourself. Take responsibility for your life and choices you made, and let go of the hate and anger against those who have hurt you. No don't forget where you came from but don't carry that burden on your back either. Jesus did that for us so we wouldn't have too, and He still does. His death was all about choices. Wonder where we would be if he chose to turn his back on us, and chose the road to save himself. Well, thank God that His only son made the choice *of sacrifice* out of love for his brothers and sisters. By doing this, he taught us that choices are all about sacrificing ourselves to make the right decisions for our love of others, and not just what is right for us alone. He also made it very clear that we have only two choices, *right, and wrong!*

I realize only I hold my *destiny*, because even though God has always been with me, it is still up to me to make the choice to let Him in and try to live by His Word. No, I'm not perfect. I am a sinner and always will be in the eyes of God, only because I am made of flesh. I will never be better than anyone else nor will they be looked upon as better than me. I won't let them ever again control me or tell me whom I have to be to fit in. I now know that I am strong and through that strength, *I will survive!*

Please, if you get nothing else from my book let it be how important it is for us to protect our children. Oh, You say you don't have children. Sure you do, there's not a child living that isn't every adult's responsibility to keep safe. If a stranger can hurt an innocent child, then a stranger can protect that very same child. Don't think because you have chosen not to have a child or you are physically unable to have a child you are exempt from protecting them, think again! This world is full of *Concrete Angels.* If you still don't get who our *Angels* are let me help you.

They are the pure innocence of this world. They are the children who are living with people whose only attention that is bestowed upon them is, pain. They are the children who are taught at a young age that this world can be a very cruel place. They are children that our society just doesn't have time to protect. They are the children that go to bed every night and pray that they will be good enough, so Mommy and Daddy will love them someday.

Yes, these are the *Concrete Angels* we see every day and wish we could help, but we just don't want to get involved or feel it is none of our business. Well, believe me, I was one these children, and so were my brothers and sisters. We do exist. Please, all I ask is that you pay attention and show a child that someone cares. Talk to them for they will never seek help from you first. The greatest gift we can give God is to take care of the greatest gift He hays given us, our children.

The End

Printed in the United States
By Bookmasters